KENSUKE'S KINGDOM

Lois ' boch

島の地図

X My first Landing place
◉ The cave where I spent my first night
----- Tracks
⊕ Where Kensuke kept outrigger

stream

His Hill

Kensuke's Cave

N

W   E

S

Kensuke's End

My End

Site of wrecked ship

My first fire where I met Kensuke

Watch Hill

KENSUKE'S KINGDOM

KENSUKE'S KINGDOM
MICHAEL MORPURGO

Illustrated by Michael Foreman

EGMONT

EGMONT

We bring stories to life

First published in Great Britain 1999 by Egmont UK Ltd
239 Kensington High Street, London W8 6SA

This colour edition published 2010

Text copyright © 1999 Michael Morpurgo

Illustrations copyright © 2010 Michael Foreman

The moral rights of the author and illustrator
have been asserted.

ISBN 978 1 4052 4856 3

1 3 5 7 9 8 6 4 2

A CIP catalogue record for this book is

available from the British Library

Printed and bound in Italy

For Graham and Isabella

*My thanks to Isabella Hutchins, Terence Buckler,
and Professor Seigo Tonimoto and his family,
for all their kind help with this book.*

目次

Contents

Chapter 1

Peggy Sue

I disappeared on the night before my twelfth birthday.
July 28 1988. Only now can I at last tell the whole
extraordinary story, the true story. Kensuke made me
promise that I would say nothing, nothing at all, until
at least ten years had passed. It was almost the last
thing he said to me. I promised, and because of that I

have had to live out a lie. I could let sleeping lies sleep on, but more than ten years have passed now. I have done school, done college, and had time to think. I owe it to my family and to my friends, all of whom I have deceived for so long, to tell the truth about my long disappearance, about how I lived to come back from the dead.

But there is another reason for speaking out now, a far, far better reason. Kensuke was a great man, a good man, and he was my friend. I want the world to know him as I knew him.

Until I was nearly eleven, until the letter came, life was just normal. There were the four of us in the house: my mother, my father, me and Stella – Stella Artois, that is, my-one-ear up and one-ear-down black and white sheepdog, who always seemed to know what was about to happen before it did. But even she could not have foreseen how that letter was going to change our lives for ever.

Thinking back, there was a regularity, a sameness about my early childhood. It was down the road each morning to 'the monkey school'. My father called it that because he said the children gibbered and screeched and hung upside down on the climbing-frame in the playground. And, anyway, I was always 'monkey face' to him – when he was in a playful mood, that is, which he often was. The school was really called St Joseph's, and I was happy there, for most of the time, anyway. After school everyday, whatever the weather, I'd be off down to the recreation ground for football with Eddie Dodds, my best friend in all the world, and Matt and Bobby and the others. It was muddy down there. Cross the ball and it would just land and stick. We had our own team, the Mudlarks we called ourselves, and we were good, too. Visiting teams seemed to expect the ball to bounce for some reason, and by the time they realised it didn't, we were often two or three goals up. We weren't so good away from home.

Every weekend I did a paper round from Mr Patel's shop on the corner. I was saving up for a mountain bike. I wanted to go mountain biking up on the moors with Eddie. The trouble was, I would keep spending what I'd saved. I'm still the same that way.

Sundays were always special, I remember. We'd go dinghy sailing, all of us, on the reservoir,

Stella Artois barking her head off at the other boats as if they'd no right to be there. My father loved it, he said, because the air was clear and clean, no brick dust – he worked down at the brickworks. He was a great do-it-yourself fanatic. There was nothing he couldn't fix, even if it didn't need fixing. So he was in his element on a boat. My mother, who worked part time in the office at the same brickworks, revelled in it, too. I remember her once, throwing back her head in the wind and breathing in deep as she sat at the tiller. 'This is it,' she cried. 'This is how life is supposed to be. Wonderful, just wonderful.' She always wore the blue cap. She was the undisputed skipper. If there was a breeze out there, she'd find it and catch it. She had a real nose for it.

We had some great days on the water. We'd go out when it was rough, when no one else would, and we'd go skimming over the waves, exhilarating in the speed of it, in the sheer joy of it. And if there wasn't a breath of wind, we didn't mind that either. Sometimes we'd be the only boat on the whole reservoir. We'd just sit and fish instead – by the way, I was better at fishing than either of them – and Stella Artois would be curled up behind us in the boat, bored with the whole thing, because there was no one to bark at.

Then the letter arrived. Stella Artois savaged it as it came through the letterbox. There were puncture holes in it and it was damp, but we could read enough. The brickworks were going to close down. They were both being made redundant.

There was a terrible silence at the breakfast table that morning. After that we never went sailing on Sundays any more. I didn't have to ask why not. They both tried to find other jobs, but there was nothing.

A creeping misery came over the house. Sometimes I'd come home and they just wouldn't be speaking. They'd argue a lot, about little niggly things – and they had never been like that. My father stopped fixing things around the house. He was scarcely ever home anyway. If he wasn't looking for a job, he'd be down in the pub. When he was home he'd just sit there flicking through endless yachting magazines and saying nothing.

I tried to stay out of the house and play football as much as I could, but then Eddie moved away because his father had found a job somewhere down south.

Football just wasn't the same without him. The Mudlarks disbanded. Everything was falling apart.

Then one Saturday I came home from my paper round and found my mother sitting at the bottom of the stairs and crying. She'd always been so strong. I'd never seen her like this before.

'Silly beggar,' she said. 'Your dad's a silly beggar, Michael, that's what he is.'

'What's he done?' I asked her.

'He's gone off,' she told me, and I thought she meant for good. 'He wouldn't hear reason, oh no. He's had this idea, he says. He wouldn't tell me what it was, only that he's sold the car, that we're moving south, and he's going to find us a place.' I was relieved, and quite pleased, really. South must be nearer to Eddie. She went on: 'If he thinks I'm leaving this house, then I'm telling you he's got another think coming.'

'Why not?' I said. 'Not much here.'

'Well there's the house, for a start. Then there's Gran, and there's school.'

'There's other schools,' I told her. She became steaming angry then, angrier than I'd ever known her.

'You want to know what was the last straw?' she

said. 'It was you, Michael, you going off on your paper round this morning. You know what your dad said? Well, I'll tell you, shall I? "Do you know something?" he says. "There's only one lousy wage coming into this house – Michael's paper money. How do you think that makes me feel, eh? My son's eleven years old. He's got a job, and I haven't." '

She steadied herself for a moment or two before she went on, her eyes filled with fierce tears. 'I'm not moving, Michael. I was born here. And I'm not going. No matter what he says, I'm not leaving.'

I was there when the phone call came a week or so later. I knew it was my father. My mother said very little, so I couldn't understand what was going on, not until she sat me down afterwards and told me.

'He sounds different, Michael. I mean, like his old self, like his very old self, like he used to be when I first knew him. He's found us a place. "Just pack your stuff and come," he says. Fareham. Somewhere near Southampton. "Right on the sea," he says. There's something very different about him, I'm telling you.'

My father did indeed seem a changed man. He was waiting for us when we got off the train, all bright-eyed again and full of laughter. He helped us with the cases. 'It's not far,' he said, ruffling my hair. 'You wait till you see it, monkey face. I've got it all sorted, the whole thing. And it's no good you trying to talk me out of it, either of you. I've made up my mind.'

'What about?' I asked him.

'You'll see,' he said.

Stella Artois bounded along ahead of us, her tail held high and happy. We all felt like that, I think.

In the end we caught a bus because the cases were too heavy. When we got off we were right by the sea. There didn't seem to be any houses anywhere, just a yachting marina.

'What are we doing here?' my mother asked.

'There's someone I want you to meet. A good friend of mine. She's called Peggy Sue. She's been looking forward to meeting you. I've told her all about you.'

My mother frowned at me in puzzlement. I wasn't any the wiser either. All I knew for certain was that he was being deliberately mysterious.

We struggled on with our suitcases, the gulls crying overhead, the yacht masts clapping around us,

We're going to do it safe, do it properly. Mum, you'll do your Yachtmaster's certificate. Oh, didn't I say? I didn't did I? You'll be the skipper, Mum. I'll be first mate and handyman. Michael, you'll be ship's boy, and Stella – well Stella can be the ship's cat.' He was full of it, breathless with excitement. 'We'll train ourselves up. Do a few trips across the channel to France, maybe over to Ireland. We'll get to know this boat like she's one of us. She's a forty-two foot. Bowman, best make, best design. Safest there is. I've done my homework. Six months' time and we'll be off round the world. It'll be the adventure of a lifetime. Our one chance. We'll never get another one. What do you think then?'

'Ex . . . cell . . . ent,' I breathed, and that was exactly what I thought.

'And I'll be skipper, you say?' my mother asked.

'Aye aye, Cap'n,' and my father laughed and gave her a mock salute.

'What about Michael's school?' she went on.

'I've thought of that, too. I asked in the local school down here. It's all arranged. We'll take all the books he'll need. I'll teach him. You'll teach him. He'll teach himself. I'll tell you something for nothing, he'll learn more in a couple of years at sea, than he ever would in that monkey school of his. Promise.'

She took a sip of tea, and then nodded slowly. 'All right,' she said, and I saw she was smiling. 'Why not? Go ahead then. Buy her. Buy the boat.'

'I already have,' said my father.

Of course it was madness. They knew it, even I knew it, but it simply didn't matter. Thinking back, it must have been a kind of inspiration driven by desperation.

Everyone warned us against it. Gran came visiting and stayed on board. It was all quite ridiculous she said, reckless, irresponsible. She was full of doom and gloom. Icebergs, hurricanes, pirates, whales, supertankers, freak waves – she heaped up horror upon horror, thinking to frighten me and so frighten off my mother and father. She succeeded in terrifying me all right, but I never showed it. What she didn't understand was that we three were already bound together now by a common lunacy. We were going, and nothing and no one could stop us. We were doing what people do in fairytales. We were going off to seek adventure.

To begin with it all happened much as my father

had planned it, except that the training took a lot longer. We soon learned that handling a forty-two foot yacht was not just dinghy sailing in a bigger boat. We were tutored by a whiskered old mariner from the yacht club, Bill Parker ('Barnacle Bill' we called him, but not to his face, of course). He had been twice round Cape Horn and done two single-handed Atlantic crossings, and he'd been across the channel 'more times than you've had hot dinners, my lad'.

To tell the truth, we none of us liked him much. He was a hard taskmaster. He treated me and Stella Artois with equal disdain. To him all animals and children were just a nuisance and, on board ship, nothing but a liability. So I kept out of his way as much as I could, and so did Stella Artois.

To be fair to him, Barnacle Bill did know his business. By the time he had finished with us, and my mother was given her certificate, we felt we could sail the *Peggy Sue* anywhere. He had inculcated in us a healthy respect for the sea but, at the same time, we were confident we could handle just about anything the sea could hurl at us.

Mind you, there were times I was scared rigid.

My father and I shared our terror together, silently. You can't pretend, I learned, with a towering green wall of sea twenty feet high bearing down on you. We went down in troughs so deep we never thought we could possibly climb out again. But we did, and the more we rode our terror, rode the waves, the more we felt sure of ourselves and of the boat around us.

My mother, though, never showed even the faintest tremor of fear. It was her and the *Peggy Sue* between them that saw us through our worst moments. She was seasick from time to time, and we never were. So that was something.

We lived close, all of us, cheek by jowl, and I soon discovered parents were more than just parents. My father became my friend, my shipmate. We came to rely on each other. And as for my mother, the truth is – and I admit it – that I didn't know she had it in her. I always known she was gritty, that she'd always keep on at a thing until she'd done it. But she worked night and day over her books and charts until she had mastered everything. She never stopped. True, she could be a bit of a tyrant if we didn't keep the boat shipshape, but neither my father nor I minded that much, though we pretended to. She was the skipper. She was going to take us round the world and back again. We had absolute confidence in her. We were proud of her. She was just brilliant. And, I have to say, the ship's boy and the first mate were pretty brilliant too on the winches, at the helm, and dab hands with the baked beans in the galley. We were a great team.

So, on September 10, 1987 – I know the date because I have the ship's log in front of me as I write – with every nook and cranny loaded with stores and provisions, we were at last ready to set sail on our grand adventure, our great odyssey.

Gran was there to wave us off, tearfully. In the end she even wanted to come with us, to visit Australia – she'd always wanted to see koalas in the wild. There were lots of our friends there too, including Barnacle Bill. Eddie Dodds came along with his father. He threw me a football as we cast off. 'Lucky mascot,' he shouted. When I looked down at it later I saw he'd signed his name all over it like a World Cup star.

Stella Artois barked her farewells at them, and at every boat we passed in the Solent. But as we were sailing out past the Isle of Wight she fell strangely quiet. Maybe she sensed, as we did, that there was no turning back now. This was not a dream. We were off round the world. It was real, really real.

Chapter 2

Water, water everywhere

They say that water covers two thirds of the earth's surface. It certainly looks like that when you're out there, and it feels like it too. Sea water, rain water – all of it is wet. I spent most of the time soaked to the skin. I wore all the right gear – the skipper always made sure of that – but somehow the wet still got through.

Down below too, everything was damp, even the sleeping-bags. Only when the sun shone and the sea had stopped its heaving, could we begin to dry out. We would haul everything out on deck, and soon the *Peggy Sue* would be dressed overall, one great washing-line from bow to stern. To be dry again was a real luxury, but we always knew it could not last for long.

You may think there was not a lot for three people to do on board, day after day, week after week. You'd be quite wrong. In daylight there was never a dull moment. I was always kept busy: taking in sail, winching in, letting out, taking my turn at the wheel – which I loved – or helping my father with his endless mending and fixing. He often needed another pair of hands to hold and steady as he drilled or hammered or screwed or sawed. I'd forever be mopping up, brewing up, washing up, drying up. I'd be lying if I said I loved it all. I didn't. But there was never a dull moment.

Only one of the crew was allowed to be idle – Stella Artois – and she was always idle. With nothing much to bark at out on the open ocean, she spent the rougher days curled up on my bed down in the cabin. When it was fine and calm, though, she'd usually be found on watch up at the bow, alert for something, anything that wasn't just sea. You could be sure that if there was anything out there she'd spot it soon enough – an escort of porpoises perhaps, diving in and out of the waves, a family of dolphins swimming alongside, so close you could reach out and touch them. Whales, sharks, even turtles – we saw them all. My mother would be taking photographs, video and still, while my father and I fought over the binoculars. But Stella Artois was in her element, a proper sheepdog again, barking her commands at the creatures of the sea, herding them up from the deep.

Annoying though she could be – she would bring her smelly wetness with her everywhere – we never once regretted bringing her along with us. She was our greatest comfort. When the sea tossed and churned us, and my mother felt like death from seasickness, she'd sit down below, white to the gills, with Stella on her lap, cuddling and being cuddled. And when I was terrified by the mountainous seas and the screaming wind, I would curl up with Stella on my bunk, bury my head in her neck and hold her tight. At times like that – and I don't suppose they were that frequent, it's just that I remember them so vividly – I always kept Eddie's football close beside me as well.

The football had become a sort of talisman for me, a lucky charm, and it really seemed to work, too. After all, every storm did blow itself out in the end and, afterwards, we were always still there, still alive and still afloat.

I had hoped my mother and father might forget all about the planned school work. And to begin with it seemed as if they had. But once we had weathered a few storms, once we were settled and well into our voyage, they sat me down and told me the unwelcome news. Like it or not, I was going to have to keep up with my schoolwork. My mother was adamant about it.

I could see that any appeals to my father would

be pointless. He just shrugged and said, 'Mum's the skipper.' And that was an end of the matter. At least at home she had been my mother and I could argue with her, but not on the *Peggy Sue*, not any more.

It was a conspiracy. Between them, they had devised an entire programme of work. There were maths course books to get through – my father would help me with that if I got stuck, he said. For geography and history I was to find out and record all I could about every country we visited as we went round the world. For environmental studies and art I was to note down and draw all the birds we saw, all the creatures and plants we came across.

My mother made a particular point of teaching me navigation, too. 'Barnacle Bill taught me,' she said, 'I'm teaching you. I know it's not on the curriculum, but so what? It could come in handy, you never know.' She taught me how to use the sextant, take compass bearings, plot a course on the chart. I had to fill in the longitude and latitude in the ship's log, every morning, every evening, without fail.

I don't think I had ever really noticed stars before. Now, whenever I was on watch in the cockpit at night, with the *Peggy Sue* on her wind-vane self-steering, the others asleep below, the stars would be my only company. Gazing up at them I felt sometimes that we were the last people alive on the whole planet. There was just us, and the dark sea about us and the millions of stars above.

It was on watch at night that I would often do my 'English'. This was my own version of the ship's log. I didn't have to show it to them, but I was encouraged to write in it every few weeks. It would be, they said, my own personal, private record of our voyage.

At school I had never been much good at writing. I could never think of what to write or how to begin. But on the *Peggy Sue* I found I could open up my log and just write. There was always so much I wanted to say. And that's the thing. I found I didn't really write it down at all. Rather, I said it. I spoke it from my head, down my arm, through my fingers and my pencil, and

on to the page. And that's how it reads to me now, all these years later, like me talking.

I'm looking at my log now. The paper is a bit crinkled and the pages are yellowed with age. My scribbly writing is a little faded, but it's mostly quite legible. What follows are just a few chosen extracts from this log. The entries are quite short, but they tell the tale. This is how I recorded our great journey. This is how it was for an eleven-year-old boy as we rode the wide oceans of the world on board the *Peggy Sue*.

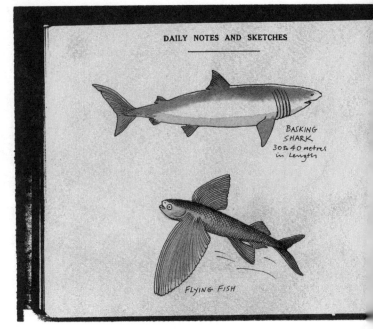

BASKING
SHARK
30 to 40 metres
in Length

FLYING FISH

LOG OF PEGGY SUE

From FAREHAM to AROUND THE WORLD! Date Oct. 11 1987

HOUR	LOG	DISTANCE MADE GOOD	COURSE	WIND DIRECTION AND FORCE	BAROMETER	LEEWAY	REMARKS

Today I saw Africa!

It was in the distance but Mum said it was definately
Africa. We're going down the west coast. Mum showed me
on the chart. The wind will take us down the coast for a few
hundred miles then across the Atlantic to South America.
It's the hottest day we've had. Dad's very red in the face, and the
top of his ears are peeling. I'm more nutty-brown, like Mum.
Saw flying fish today and so did Stella.

Then Mum spotted a shark off the port bow, a basking shark,
she thought. I got the binoculars out but I never saw it.

She said I had to write it down in my note book anyway,
and then draw it. I looked them up. They're massive,
but don't eat people, just fish and plankton.

I like doing my drawings. My best one so far is a flying fish.
I sent a card to Eddie from the Cape Verde Islands.
I wish he could be here. We'd have a real laugh.
Stella loves to chase the football around the cabin,
and pounce on it. She'll puncture it one day, I know she will.

| LATITUDE | LONGITUDE | | | | ENGINE USED | Hrs. | Mins. |

Chapter 3

Ship's Log

September 20

*It's five in the morning. I'm on watch in the cockpit
and no one else is awake. We left Southampton ten
days ago now. The Channel was full of tankers. There
were dozens of them going up and down. So, either
Mum or Dad took turns on watch the first two nights.
They wouldn't let me. I don't know why not. There*

wasn't any fog, and I can see as well as they can.

We were planning on sailing about 200 miles a day, that's about eight knots. But in the first week we were lucky if we made fifty miles a day.

Barnacle Bill warned us about the Bay of Biscay, so we were expecting it to be bad, and it was. Force 9 gale. Force 10 sometimes. We were slammed about all over the place. I thought we'd sink. I really did. Once, when we came up on to the top of a wave, I saw the bow of the *Peggy Sue* pointing straight up at the moon. It was like she was going to take off. Then we were hurled down the other side so fast I was sure we were going to the bottom. It was bad. I mean it was horrible, really horrible. But the *Peggy Sue* didn't fall apart, and we made it to Spain.

Mum gets quite snappy with us sometimes when we don't do things right. Dad doesn't seem to mind, not out here, not at sea. He just winks at me and we get on with it. They play a lot of chess together, when it's calm enough. Dad's winning so far, five games to three. Mum says she's not bothered, but she is. I can tell.

We only spent a couple of days in La Coruña.

Mum slept a lot. She was really tired. Dad did some work on the rudder cable while we were there. He's still not happy with it, though. We set off for the Azores two days ago.

Yesterday was the best day we've had for sailing. Strong breeze, blue sky, and warm sun to dry things out. My blue shorts blew off the washing line into the sea. It doesn't matter. I never liked them much anyway. We saw gannets slicing into the sea all around us this afternoon. Really excellent. Stella Artois went mad.

I'm fed up with baked beans already, and there's still stacks of them down below.

October 11
Today I saw Africa! It was in the distance but Mum said it was definitely Africa. We're going down the west coast. Mum showed me on the chart. The wind will

take us down the coast for a few hundred miles then across the Atlantic to South America. We mustn't drift off course, else we'll get into the Doldrums. There's no wind there at all, and we could just sit there becalmed for weeks, for ever maybe.

It's the hottest day we've had. Dad's very red in the face, and the tops of his ears are peeling. I'm more nutty brown, like Mum.

Saw flying fish early this morning and so did Stella. Then Mum spotted a shark off the port bow. A basking shark, she thought. I got the binoculars out, but I never saw it. She said I had to write it down in my notebook anyway, and then draw it. I looked them up. They're massive, but they don't eat people, just fish and plankton. I like doing my drawings. My best one so far is a flying fish.

I sent a card to Eddie from the Cape

BASKING SHARK
30 a 40 metres
in length

FLYING FISH

Verde Islands. I wish he could be here. We'd have a real laugh.

Stella loves to chase the football round the cabin, and pounce on it. She'll puncture it one day, I know she will.

Dad's been a bit gloomy, and Mum's gone to lie down. She's got a headache. I think they've had a bit of a tiff. Don't know what about exactly, but I think it's about chess.

November 16

We've just left Recife. That's in Brazil. We were there four days. We had a lot of repairs to do on the boat. Something was wrong with the wind generator and the rudder cable's still sticking.

I've played football in Brazil! Did you hear that, Eddie? I've played football in Brazil, and with your lucky football. Dad and me were just having a kick about on the beach, and before we knew it we had a dozen kids joining in. It was a proper game. Dad set it up. We picked sides. I called my side Mudlarks and he called his Brazil, so they all wanted to play on his side, of course.

But Mum joined in on my side and we won. Mudlarks 5 – Brazil 3. Mum invited them back for a Coke on board afterwards. Stella growled at them and bared her teeth, so we had to shut her down in the cabin. They tried out their English on us. They only knew two words: 'Goal' and 'Manchester United'. That's three, I suppose.

Mum had the films developed. There's one of some leaping dolphins, another of me at the winch. Mum at the wheel, another of Dad hauling down the

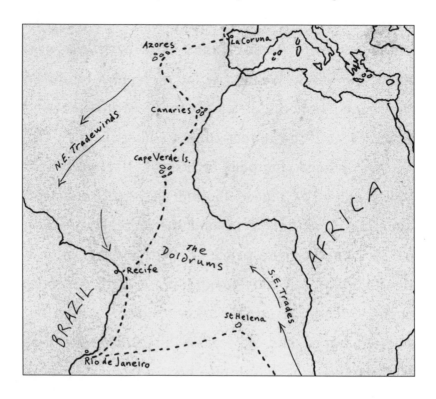

mainsail and making a right mess of it. There's one of me diving off a rock into the sea when we stopped in the Canaries. There's one of Dad fast asleep and sunbathing on deck and Mum giggling. She's about to dribble the sun cream all over his tummy. (I took that one, my best photo.) Then there's one of me doing my maths, sulking and sticking my tongue out.

December 25

Christmas Day at sea. Dad found some carols on the radio. We had crackers, all of them a bit soggy so none of them cracked, and we had the Christmas pudding Gran made for us. I gave them a drawing each – my flying fish for Dad and one of the skipper, in her hat, at the wheel for Mum. They gave me a really neat knife they'd bought in Rio. So I gave a coin back. You're supposed to do that. It's for luck.

When we were in Rio we gave the *Peggy Sue* a good scrub down. She was looking a bit manky inside and outside, but she's not any more. We took on a lot of stores and water for the long haul to South Africa. Mum says we're doing fine, just so long as we keep south, so long as we stay in the west-to-east South Atlantic current.

We passed south of an island called St Helena a few days ago. No need to stop. Nothing much there, except it's the place where Napoleon was exiled. He died there. Lonely place to die. So, of course, I had to do a history project on Napoleon. I had to look him up in the encyclopaedia and write about him. It was quite interesting, really, but I

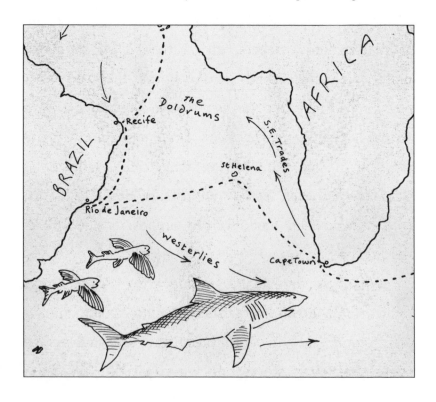

didn't tell them that.

Stella's sulking on my bunk. Maybe it's because no one gave her a Christmas present. I offered her a taste of Gran's Christmas pudding, but she hardly gave it a sniff. Can't say I blame her.

I saw a sail today, another yacht. We shouted Happy Christmas and waved, and Stella barked her head off, but they were too far away. When the sail disappeared, the sea felt suddenly very empty.

Mum won the chess this evening. She's ahead now, twenty-one games to twenty. Dad said he let her win because it was Christmas. They joke about it, but they both want to win.

January 1, 1989
Africa again! Cape Town. Table Mountain. And this time we're not just sailing by — we're going to put in there. They told me this evening. They didn't want to tell me before in case we couldn't afford it, but we can. We're going to stay for a couple of weeks, maybe more. We're going to see elephants and lions in the wild. I can't believe it. I don't think they can either. When they told me, they were like

a couple of kids, all laughing and happy. They were never like this at home. These days they really smile at each other.

Mum's getting stomach cramps. Dad wants her to see a doctor in Cape Town, but she won't. I reckon it's the baked beans. The good news is the baked beans have at last run out. The bad news is we had sardines for supper. Eeeyuk!

February 7

We're hundreds of miles out in the Indian Ocean, and then this happens. Stella hardly ever comes up on deck unless it's flat calm. I don't know why she came up. I don't know why she was there. We were all busy, I suppose. Dad was brewing up down in the galley, and Mum was at the wheel. I was doing one of my navigation lessons, taking bearings with the sextant. The *Peggy Sue* was pitching and rolling a bit. I had to steady myself. I looked up and I saw Stella up at the bow of the boat. One moment she was just standing there, the next she was gone.

We had practised the 'man overboard' drill dozens of times back in the Solent with Barnacle

Bill. Shout and point. Keep shouting. Keep pointing. Turn into the wind. Get the sails down quick. Engine on. By the time Dad had the mainsail and the jib down, we were already heading back towards her. I was doing the pointing, and the shouting too. She was paddling for her life in the green of a looming wave. Dad was leaning over the side and reaching for her, but he didn't have his safety harness on and Mum was going mad. She was trying to bring the boat in as close and as slow

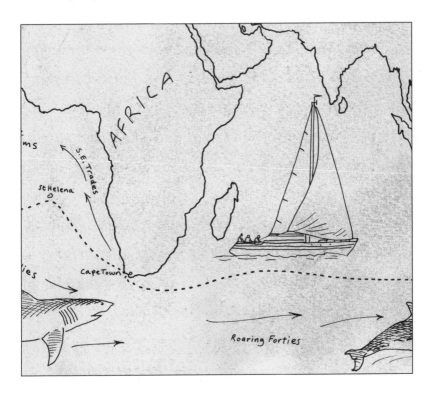

as she could, but a wave took Stella away from us at the last moment. We had to turn and come back again. All the time I was pointing and shouting.

Three times we came in but each time we passed her by. Either we were going too fast or she was out of reach. She was weak by now. She was hardly paddling. She was going under. We had one last chance. We came in again, perfectly this time and close enough for Dad to be able to reach out and grab her. Between the three of us we managed to haul Stella back into the boat by her collar, by her tail. I got a, 'Well done, monkey face,' from Dad, and Dad got a huge rollicking from Mum for not wearing his safety harness. Dad just put his arms round her and she cried. Stella shook herself and went below as if nothing at all had happened.

Mum has made a strict rule. Stella Artois is never to go out on deck – whatever the weather – without a safety harness clipped on, like the rest of us. Dad's going to make one for her.

I still dream of the elephants in South Africa. I loved how slow they are, and thoughtful.

I loved their wise weepy eyes. I can still see those snooty giraffes looking down at me and the lion cub sleeping with his mother's tail in his mouth. I did lots of drawings and I keep looking at them to remind me. The sun in Africa is so big, so red.

Australia next. Kangaroos and possums and wombats. Uncle John's going to meet us in Perth. I've seen photos of him but I've never met him. Dad said this evening he's only a distant uncle. 'Very distant,' Mum said, and they both laughed. I didn't get the joke till I thought about it again when I came on watch.

The stars are so bright, and Stella was saved. I think I'm happier than I have been all my life.

April 3

Off Perth, Australia. Until today it has been nothing but empty ocean all the way from Africa. I love it more and more when it's just us and *Peggy Sue* and the sea. We all do, I think. But then, when we sight land we always get so excited. When we saw Australia for the first time we hugged each other and jumped up and down. It's like we're the first sailors ever to discover it. Stella Artois barked at us as if we were mad as hatters, which we probably are. But we've done it. We've sailed all the way from England to Australia. That's halfway round the world. And we did it on our own.

Mum's been getting her stomach cramps again. She's definitely going to see a doctor in Australia. She's promised us and we'll make her keep to it.

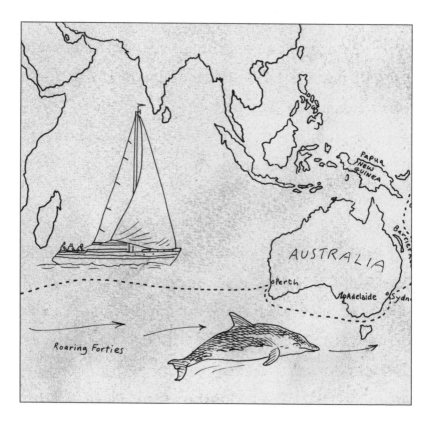

May 28

At sea again after nearly six weeks with Uncle John. We thought we were going to stay in Perth for just a few days, but he said we had to see Australia properly while we were there. He took us to stay with his family on a huge farm. Thousands of sheep. He's got masses of horses, so I went riding a lot with my two little cousins, Beth and Liza. They're only seven and eight, but they could really ride. They called me Mikey, and by the time we left they both wanted to marry me. We're going to be penpals instead.

I saw a snake called a Copperhead. Uncle John said it could have killed me if I'd trodden on it. He told me to watch out for Redback spiders in the toilet. I didn't go to the toilet very often after that.

They called us their 'pommy cousins' and we had barbeques every evening. They gave us a great time. But I was happy to get back to the *Peggy Sue*. I missed her while I was gone, like I miss Eddie. I've been sending him cards, funny animal cards, if I can find them. I sent him one of a wombat. I saw a wombat too, and hundreds of possums and loads of kangaroos. And they've got white cockatoos in Australia like we've got sparrows at home – millions of them.

But out here it's gulls again. Wherever we've been in the world there's always gulls. The plan is we're going to put in at Sydney, explore the Barrier Reef for a bit, then go through the Coral Sea and up towards Papua New Guinea.

Mum's stomach cramps are much better. The doctor in Australia said that it was most probably something she'd eaten. Anyway, she's better now.

It's really hot and heavy. It's calm too. No wind. We're hardly moving. I can't see any clouds, but I'm sure a storm is coming. I can feel it.

July 28

I look around me. It's a dark, dark night. No moon. No stars. But it's calm again, at last. I'll be twelve tomorrow, but I don't think anyone except me will remember it.

We've had a terrible time, far worse even than in the Bay of Biscay. Ever since we left Sydney, it's been just storm after storm, and each one blows us further north across the Coral Sea. The rudder cable has snapped. Dad's done what he can, but it's still not right. The self-steering doesn't work any more, so someone's got to be at the wheel all the time. And that means Dad or me, because Mum is sick. It's her stomach cramps again, but they're a lot worse. She doesn't want to eat at all. All she has is sugared water. She hasn't been able to look at the charts for three days. Dad wants to put out a May Day call, but Mum won't let him. She says that's giving in, and she's never giving in. Dad and I have been doing the navigation together. We've

been doing our best, but I don't think we know where we are any more.

They're both asleep down below. Dad's really wiped out. I'm at the wheel in the cockpit. I've got Eddie's football with me. It's been lucky for us so far. And now we really need it. We need Mum to get better, or we're in real trouble. I don't know if we could stand another storm.

Thank God it's calm. It'll help Mum to sleep. You can't sleep when you're being slammed about all the time.

It is so dark out there. Black. Stella's barking. She's up by the bow. She hasn't got her harness clipped on.

Those were the last words I ever wrote in my log. After that it's just empty pages.

I tried calling Stella first, but she wouldn't come. So I left the wheel and went forward to bring her back. I took the ball with me to sweeten her in, to tempt her away from the bow of the boat.

I crouched down. 'Come on, Stella,' I said, rolling the ball from hand to hand. 'Come and get the ball.' I felt the boat turn a little in the wind, and I knew then I shouldn't have left the wheel. The ball rolled away from me quite suddenly. I lunged after it, but it was gone over the side before I could grab it. I lay there on the deck watching it bob away into the darkness. I was furious with myself for being so silly.

I was still cursing myself when I thought I heard the sound of singing. Someone was singing out there in the darkness. I called out but no one replied. So that was what Stella had been barking at.

I looked again for my ball, but by now it had disappeared. That ball had been very precious to me, precious to all of us. I knew then I had just lost a great deal more than a football.

I was angry with Stella. The whole thing had been her fault. She was still barking. I couldn't hear the singing any more. I called her again, whistled her in. She wouldn't come. I got to my feet and went forward. I took her by the collar and pulled. She would not be moved. I couldn't drag her all the way back, so I bent down to pick her up. She was still reluctant. Then I had her in my arms, but she was struggling.

I heard the wind above me in the sails. I remember thinking: this is silly, you haven't got your safety harness on, you haven't got your lifejacket on, you shouldn't be doing this. Then the boat veered violently and I was thrown sideways. With my arms full I had no time to grab the guard rail. We were in the cold of the sea before I could even open my mouth to scream.

Chapter 4

Gibbons
and ghosts

The terrors came fast, one upon another. The lights
of the *Peggy Sue* went away into the dark of the
night, leaving me alone in the ocean, alone with the
certainty that they were already too far away, that

my cries for help could not possibly be heard. I thought then of the sharks cruising the black water beneath me – scenting me, already searching me out, homing in on me – and I knew there could be no hope. I would be eaten alive. Either that or I would drown slowly. Nothing could save me.

I trod water, frantically searching the impenetrable darkness about me for something, anything to swim towards. There was nothing.

Then a sudden glimpse of white in the sea. The breaking of a wave perhaps. But there were no waves. Stella! It had to be. I was so thankful, so relieved not to be all alone. I called out and swam towards her. She would keep bobbing away from me, vanishing, reappearing, then vanishing again. She had seemed so near, but it took several minutes of hard swimming before I came close enough to reach out and touch her. Only then did I realise my mistake. Stella's head was mostly black. This was white. It was my football. I grabbed it and clung on, feeling the unexpected and wonderful buoyancy of it. I held on, treading water and calling for Stella. There was no answer. I called and I called. But every time I opened my mouth now, the seawater washed in. I had to give her up. I had to save myself if I could.

There was little point in wasting energy by trying to swim. After all, I had nowhere to swim to. Instead, I would simply float. I would cling to my football, tread water gently and wait for the *Peggy Sue* to come back. Sooner or later they had to discover I was overboard. Sooner or later they would come looking for me. I mustn't kick too much, just enough to keep my chin above the water, no more. Too much movement would attract the sharks. Morning must come soon. I had to hang on till then. I had to. The water wasn't that cold. I had my football. I had a chance.

I kept telling myself that over and over again. But the world stayed stubbornly black about me, and I could feel the water slowly chilling me to death. I tried singing to stop myself from shivering, to take my mind off the sharks. I sang every song I could remember, but after a while I'd forget the words. Always I came back to the only song I was sure I could finish: 'Ten Green Bottles'. I sang it out loud again and again. It reassured me to hear the sound of my own voice. It made me feel less alone in the sea. And always I looked for the grey glint of dawn, but it would not come and it would not come.

Eventually I fell silent and my legs just would not kick any more. I clung to my football, my head drifting into sleep. I knew I mustn't, but I couldn't help myself. My hands kept slipping off the ball. I was fast losing the last of my strength. I would go down, down to the bottom of the sea and lie in my grave amongst the seaweed and the sailors' bones and the shipwrecks.

The strange thing was that I didn't really mind. I didn't care, not any more. I floated away into sleep, into my dreams. And in my dream I saw a boat gliding towards me, silent over the sea. The *Peggy Sue*! Dear, dear *Peggy Sue*. They had come back for me. I knew they would. Strong arms grabbed me. I was hauled upwards and out of the water. I lay there on the deck, gasping for air like a landed fish.

Someone was bending over me, shaking me, talking to me. I could not understand a word that was being said. But it didn't matter. I felt Stella's hot breath on my face, her tongue licking my ear. She was safe. I was safe. All was well.

I was woken by a howling, like the howling of a gale through the masts. I looked about me. There were no masts above me, there were no sails. No movement under me either, no breath of wind. Stella Artois was barking, but some way off. I was not on a boat at all, but lying stretched out on sand. The howling became a screaming, a fearful crescendo of screeching that died away in its own echoes.

I sat up. I was on a beach, a broad white sweep of sand, with trees growing thick and lush behind me right down to the beach. Then I saw Stella prancing about in the shallows. I called her and she came bounding up out of the sea to greet me, her tail circling wildly. When all the leaping and licking and hugging were done, I struggled to my feet.

I was weak all over. I looked all about me. The wide blue sea was as empty as the cloudless sky above. No *Peggy Sue*. No boat. Nothing. No one. I called again and again for my mother and my father. I called until the tears came and I could call no more, until I knew there was no point. I stood there for some time trying to work out how I had got here, how it was that I'd survived. I had such confused memories, of being picked up, of being on board the *Peggy Sue*. But I knew now I couldn't have been. I must have dreamed it, dreamed the whole thing. I must have clung to my football and kept myself afloat until I was washed up. I thought of my football then, but it was nowhere to be seen.

Stella, of course, was unconcerned about all the whys and wherefores. She kept bringing me sticks to throw, and would go galloping after them into the sea without a care in the world.

Then came the howling again from the trees, and the hackles went up on Stella's neck. She charged up the beach barking and barking, until she was sure she had silenced the last of the echoes. It was a musical, plaintive howling this time, not at all menacing. I thought I recognised it. I had heard howling like it once before on a visit to London Zoo. Gibbons, 'funky gibbons', my father had called them. I still don't know why to this day. But I loved the sound of the word 'funky'. Perhaps that was why I remembered what they were. 'It's only gibbons,' I told Stella, 'just funky gibbons. They won't hurt us.' But I couldn't be at all sure I was right.

From where I now stood I could see that the forest grew more sparsely up the side of a great hill some way inland, and it occurred to me then that if I could reach the bare rocky outcrop at the summit, I would be able to see further out to sea. Or perhaps there'd be some house or farm further inland, or maybe a road, and I could find someone to help. But if I left the beach and they came back looking for me, what then? I decided I would have to take that chance.

I set off at a run, Stella Artois at my heels, and soon found myself in the cooling shade of the forest. I discovered a narrow track going uphill, in the right direction, I thought. So I followed it, only slowing to a walk when the hill became too steep. The forest was alive with creatures. Birds cackled and screeched high above me, and always the howling wailed and wafted through the trees, but more distantly now.

It wasn't the sounds of the forest that bothered me, though, it was the eyes. I felt as if I was being watched by a thousand inquisitive eyes. I think Stella did, too, for she had been strangely quiet ever since we entered the forest, constantly glancing up at me for reassurance and comfort. I did my best to give it, but she could sense that I, too, was frightened.

What had seemed at first to be a short hike now felt more like a great expedition into the interior. We emerged exhausted from the trees, clambered laboriously up a rocky scree and stood at long last on the peak.

The sun was blazing down. I had not really felt the burning heat of it until then. I scanned the horizon. If there was a sail somewhere out there in the haze, I could not see it. And then it came to me that even if I were to see a sail, what could I do? I couldn't light a fire. I had no matches. I knew about cavemen rubbing sticks together, but I had never tried it. I looked all round me now. Sea. Sea.

Sea. Nothing but sea on all sides. I was on an island. I was alone.

The island looked perhaps two or three miles in length, no more. It was shaped a bit like an elongated peanut, but longer at one end than the other. There was a long swathe of brilliant white beach on both sides of the island, and at the far end another hill, the slopes steeper and more thickly wooded, but not so high as mine. With the exception of these twin peaks the entire island seemed to be covered with forest. So far as I could see there was no sign of any human life. Even then, as I stood there, that first morning, filled with apprehension at the terrifying implications of my dreadful situation, I remember thinking how wonderful it was, a green jewel of an island framed in white, the sea all about it a silken shimmering blue. Strangely, perhaps comforted somehow by the extraordinary beauty of the place, I was not at all down-hearted. On the contrary I felt strangely elated. I was alive. Stella Artois was alive. We had survived.

I sat down in the shadow of a great rock. The gibbons set up a renewed chorus of howling and hooting in the forest, and a flock of raucous birds clattered up out of the canopy of the trees below us and flew off across the island to settle in the trees on the hillside opposite.

'We'll be all right,' I told Stella. 'Mum and Dad, they'll come back for us. They're bound to. They will. They will. Mum'll get better and they'll come back. She won't leave us here. She'll find us, you'll see. All we've got to do is keep a look out for them – and stay alive. Water, we'll need water. But so do those monkeys, right? We've just got to find it, that's all. And there must be food too – fruit or nuts, something. Whatever it is that they eat, we'll eat.'

It helped to speak my thoughts out loud to Stella, helped to calm the panic that came over me now in waves. More than anything, it was Stella's companionship that helped me through those first hours on the island.

It seemed to make sense not to plunge at once into the forest looking for water – to be honest I was too frightened anyway – but rather to explore the shoreline first. I might come across a stream or river flowing out into the sea and, with a bit of luck, on the way I might well find something I could eat as well.

I set off in good spirits, leaping down the scree like a mountain goat. Where monkeys lived, I reasoned, we could live. I kept telling myself that. I soon discovered that the track down through the trees was bereft of all edible vegetation. I did see fruit of sorts, what looked to me like fruit, anyway. There were coconuts up there too, but the trees were all impossible to climb. Some rose a hundred feet, some two hundred feet from the forest floor – I had never seen such giant trees.

At least the intertwining canopy did provide welcome relief from the heat of the day. All the same, I was becoming desperately parched now, and so was Stella. She padded alongside me all the way, her tongue hanging. She kept giving me baleful looks whenever our eyes met. There was no comfort I could give her.

We found our beach once again and set off round the island, keeping wherever possible to the edge of the forest, to the shade. Still we found no stream. Again, I saw plenty of fruit, but always too high, and the trees were always too smooth, too sheer to climb. I found plenty of coconuts on the ground, but always cracked open and empty inside.

When the beach petered out, we had to strike off into the forest itself. Here too I found a narrow track to follow. The forest became impenetrable at this point, dark and menacing. There was no howling any more, but something infinitely more sinister: the shiver of leaves, the cracking of twigs, sudden surreptitious rustlings, and they were near me, all around me. I knew, I was quite sure now, that eyes were watching us. We were being followed.

I hurried on, swallowing my fear as best I could. I thought of the gibbons I had seen back in the zoo and tried to persuade myself how harmless they had looked. They'd leave us alone, they'd never attack us. They weren't man-eaters. But as the rustlings came ever closer, ever more threatening, I found it harder and harder to convince myself. I began to run, and I kept running until the track brought us out on to rocks, into the blessed light of day, and there was the sea again.

This end of the island appeared to be littered with massive boulders that lay like tumbled cliffs all along the coast. We leaped from one to the other, and all the while I kept a keen eye out for the trickle of a stream coming down through the rocks from the forest above, but I found none.

I was exhausted by now. I sat down to rest, my mouth dry, my head throbbing. I was racked with desperate thoughts. I would die of thirst. I would be torn limb from limb by the monkeys.

Stella's eyes looked up into mine. 'There's got to be water,' I told her. 'There's got to be.' So, said her eyes, what are you doing sitting here feeling sorry for yourself?

I forced myself to my feet and went on. The seawater in the rockpools was so cool, so tempting. I tasted it, but it was salty and brackish. I spat it out at once. You went mad if you drank it. I knew that much.

The sun was already low in the sky by the time we reached the beach on the other side of the island – we were only about halfway round by my reckoning. This place was so much bigger than it had seemed from high up on the hill that morning. Despite all my searching, I had found no water, nothing to eat. I could go no further, and neither could Stella. She lay stretched out beside me on the sand, panting her heart out. We would have to stay where we were for the night. I thought of going into the forest a little way to sleep on ground under the trees – I could make a nest of soft dead leaves, the jungle floor was thick with them – but I dared not venture in, not with the shadow of night falling fast over the island.

The howling had started up again far away in the forest, a last mellifluous evensong, a chanting that went on and on until darkness covered the island. Insects (that is what I presumed they were anyway) whirred and whined from the forest. There was hollow tapping, like a frantic woodpecker. There was scraping, scratching, and a grunting grating noise that sounded like frogs. The whole orchestra of the jungle was tuning up. But it wasn't the sounds that frightened me, it was those phantom eyes. I wanted to be as far as possible from those eyes. I found a small cave at one end of the beach with a dry sandy floor. I lay down and tried to sleep, but Stella would not let me. She whined at me in the pain of her hunger and thirst, so that I slept only fitfully.

The jungle droned and cackled and croaked, and all night long the mosquitoes were at me too. They whined in my ears and drove me mad. I held my hands over my ears to shut out the sound of them. I curled myself round Stella, tried to forget where I was, to lose myself in my dreams. I remembered then that it was my birthday, and thought of my last birthday back at home with Eddie and Matt, and the barbecue we'd had in the garden, how the sausages had smelled so good. I slept at last.

The next morning I woke cold and hungry and shivering, and bitten all over. It took me some moments to remember where I was, and all that had happened to me. I was suddenly overwhelmed by one cruel reality after another: my utter aloneness, my separation from my mother and father, and the dangers all around me.

I cried aloud in my misery, until I saw that Stella was gone. I ran out of the cave. She was nowhere to be seen. I called for her. I listened for her, but only the gibbons howled in reply. Then I turned and saw her. She was up on the rocks high above my cave, half hidden from me, but even so I could see that her head was down. She was clearly intent on something. I clambered up to find out what it was.

I heard her drinking before I got there, lapping rhythmically, noisily, as she always did. She did not even look up as I approached. That was when I saw that she was drinking from a bowl, a battered tin bowl. Then I noticed something strange up on a flat shelf of rock above her.

I left Stella to her water feast and climbed up further to investigate. Another bowl of water and, beside it, palm leaves laid out on the rock and half covered by an upturned tin. I sat down and drank the water without pause for breath. Water had never tasted so wonderful to me as it did then. Still gasping, I lifted aside the tin. Fish! Thin strips of translucent white fish, dozens of them, laid out neatly in rows on the palm leaves, and five, six, seven small red bananas. Red bananas!

I ate the fish first, savouring each precious strip. But even as I ate I was looking around me, looking for a telltale trembling of leaves at the edge of the forest, or for a trail of footprints in the sand. I could see none. Yet someone had brought this to me. Someone must be there, someone must be watching me. I wasn't sure whether to be fearful at this revelation or overjoyed.

Stella interrupted my thoughts. She was whimpering pitifully at me from the rock below, and I knew it wasn't love or comfort she was after. She caught every strip of fish I threw her, snaffled it in one gulp and waited for the next, head on one side, one ear pricked. After that it was one for me, one for her. Her beseeching eyes would not let me do otherwise.

The fish was raw, but I did not mind. I was too hungry to mind, and so was Stella. I kept the red bananas all to myself. I ate every single one of them. They weren't at all like bananas back home, but much sweeter altogether, much juicier, much more delicious. I could have eaten a dozen more.

Once I had finished I stood up and scanned the forest. My benefactor, whoever he or she was, had to be somewhere close by. I was sure I had nothing to fear. I had to make some kind of contact. I put my hands to my mouth and called out again and again: 'Thank you! Thank you! Thank you!' My words echoed round the island. Suddenly the forest was alive again with noise, a great cacophony of singing and hooting and howling and cawing and croaking. Stella barked wildly back at it. As for me, I felt suddenly exhilarated, elated, ecstatically happy. I jumped up and down laughing and laughing, until my laughter turned to tears of joy. I was not alone on this island! Whoever was here must be friendly. Why else would they have fed us? But why wouldn't they show themselves?

They would have to come back for the bowls, I thought. I would leave a message. I found a sharp stone, knelt down and scraped out my message on the rock beside the bowls: *'Thank you. My name is Michael. I fell off a boat. Who are you?'*

After that, I determined to remain on the beach

all that day, and stay close to my cave and the rock above where the fish had been left for us. I would keep it always in sight, so that I would at least be able to see who it was that had helped me.

Stella ran on ahead of me down into the sea, barking at me, inviting me to join her. I didn't need any persuading. I plunged and cavorted and whooped and splashed, but through all my antics she just cruised steadily on. She always looked so serious when she swam, chin up and paddling purposefully.

The sea was balmy and calm, barely a ripple of wave to be seen. I didn't dare go out of my depth – I'd had quite enough of that for a lifetime. I came out clean and refreshed and invigorated, a new person. The sea was a great healer. My bites were still there, but they did not burn any more.

I decided I would explore further along the beach, right to the end if I could, just so long as I could keep my cave in view all the time. There were shells here, millions of them, golden and pink thrown up in long lines all along the beach. Before long I came across what seemed at some distance away like a flat wedge of rock protruding only very slightly from the sand. Stella was scrabbling excitedly at the edge of it. It turned out not to be a rock at all, but a long sheet of rusted metal – clearly all that was left of the side of a ship's hull, now sunk deep in the sand. I wondered what ship it was, how long ago she had been wrecked. Had some terrible storm driven her on to the island? Had there been any survivors? Could any of them still be here? I knelt down in the sand and ran my hand along it. I noticed then a fragment of clear glass lying in the sand nearby from a bottle perhaps. It was hot to touch, too hot to handle.

It came to me in a flash. Eddie had showed me how to do it. We'd tried it in the playground at school, hiding behind the dustbins where no one could see us. A piece of paper, a bit of glass and the sun. We had made fire! I didn't have any paper, but leaves would do. I ran up the beach and gathered whatever I could find from under the trees: bits of cane, twigs, all sorts of leaves – paper thin, tinder dry. I made a small pile on the sand and sat down beside it. I held my piece of glass close to the leaves and angled it to the sun. I had to keep it still, quite still, and wait for the first wisp of smoke.

If only I could get a fire lit, if only I could keep it alight, then I could sleep by it at night – it would keep the flies away, and the animals away, too. And, sooner or later, a ship had to come by. Someone would spot the smoke.

I sat and I sat. Stella came over to bother me – she wanted to play – but I pushed her away. In the end she went off and sulked, stretching out with a sigh under the shade of the palm trees. The sun was roasting hot, but still nothing happened. My arm was beginning to ache, so I arranged a frame of twigs above the leaves, laid the glass across it, then crouched by it and waited. Still nothing.

All of a sudden Stella sprang up from her sleep, a deep growl in her throat. She turned and ran down towards me, wheeling round to bark her fury at the forest. Then I saw what it was that had disturbed her.

A shadow under the trees moved and came lumbering out into the sunlight towards us. A monkey, a giant monkey. Not a gibbon at all. It moved slowly on all fours, and was brown, ginger-brown. An orang-utan, I was sure of it. He sat down just a few feet from me and considered me. I dared not move. When he'd seen enough, he scratched his neck casually, turned and made his way on all fours slowly back into the forest. Stella went on growling long after he had gone.

So there were orang-utans here as well as gibbons. Or perhaps it was orang-utans that made the howling noise and not gibbons at all. Maybe I'd been wrong all along. I'd seen a Clint Eastwood film once with an orang-utan. That one, I remembered, had been friendly enough. I just hoped this one would be the same.

Then I saw smoke. I smelled smoke. There was a glow in amongst my pile of leaves. I crouched down at once and blew on it gently. The glow became flames. I put on a few more leaves, then a dry twig or two, then some bigger ones. I had a fire! I had a fire!

I dashed into the forest and collected all the debris, all the dried-up coconut shells, all the wood I could find. Back and forth I went until my fire was roaring and crackling like an inferno. Sparks were flying high into the air. Smoke was rising into the trees behind me. I knew I could not rest now, that the fire would need still more wood, bigger wood, branches even. I would have to fetch and carry until I was quite certain I had enough to keep it going, and enough in reserve.

Stella, I noticed, would not come with me into the forest, but stayed waiting for me by the fire. I knew well enough why. I kept a wary eye out for the orang-utan myself, but I was too intent on my fire now to worry much about him.

My pile of wood was huge by now, but all the same I went back into the forest one last time, just in case the fire burned itself out quicker than I expected. I had to go deeper into the forest, so it took a while.

I was coming out of the trees, loaded with wood up to my chin, when I realised there was much less smoke coming from the fire than there had been before, and no flames at all. Then, through the smoke, I saw him, the orang-utan. He was crouching down and scooping sand on to my fire. He stood up and came towards me, now out of the smoke. He was not an orang-utan at all. He was a man.

Chapter 5

I, Kensuke

He was diminutive, no taller than me, and as old a man as I had ever seen. He wore nothing but a pair of tattered breeches bunched at the waist, and there was a large knife in his belt. He was thin, too. In places – under his arms, round his neck and his midriff – his copper brown skin lay in folds about him, almost as if he'd shrunk inside it. What little hair he had on his head and his chin was long and wispy and white.

I could see at once that he was very agitated, his chin trembling, his heavily hooded eyes accusing and angry. '*Dameda*! *Dameda*!' he screeched at me. This whole body was shaking with fury. I backed away as he scuttled up the beach towards me, gesticulating wildly with his stick, and haranguing me as he came. Ancient and skeletal he may have been, but he was moving fast, running almost. '*Dameda*! *Dameda*!' I had no idea what he was saying. It sounded Chinese or Japanese, maybe.

I was about to turn and run when Stella, who, strangely, had not barked at him at all, suddenly left my side and went bounding off towards him. Her hackles were not up. She was not growling. To my astonishment she greeted him like a long lost friend. He was no more than a few feet away from me when he stopped. We stood looking at each other in silence for a few moments. He was leaning on his stick, trying to catch his breath. 'Americajin? Americajin? American? *Eikokujin*? British?'

'Yes,' I said, relieved to have understood

something at last. 'English, I'm English.'

It seemed a struggle for him to get the words out. 'No good. Fire, no good. You understand? No fire.' He seemed less angry now.

'But my mother, my father, they might see it, see the smoke.' It was plain he didn't understand me. So I pointed out to sea, by way of explanation. 'Out there. They're out there. They'll see the fire. They'll come and fetch me.'

Instantly he became aggressive again. *'Dameda!'* he shrieked, waving his stick at me. 'No fire!' I thought for a moment he was going to attack me, but he did not. Instead he began to rake through the sand at my feet with his stick. He was drawing the outline of something, jabbering incomprehensibly all the time. It looked like some kind of a fruit at first, a nut perhaps, a peanut. Now I understood. It was a map of the island. When it was done he fell on his knees beside it, and piled up mounds of sand, one at each end – the two hills. Then, very deliberately, he etched out a straight line, top to bottom, cutting the smaller end of the island off from the larger one.

'You, boy. You here,' he said, pointing back

towards my cave at the end of the beach. 'You.' And he stabbed his finger in the mound of sand that was my hill. Then across the whole of the sand map he began to write something. The lettering was not letters at all, but symbols – all kinds of ticks and pyramids and crosses and horizontal lines and slashes and squiggles – and he wrote it all backwards, in columns, from right to left.

He sat back on his haunches and tapped his chest. 'Kensuke. I, Kensuke. My island.' And he brought his hand down sharply like a chopper, separating the island in two. 'I, Kensuke. Here. You, boy. Here.' I was already in no doubt as to what he meant. Suddenly he was on his feet again waving me away with his stick. 'Go, boy. No fire. *Dameda*. No fire. You understand?'

I did not argue, but walked away at once. When, after a while, I dared to look back, he was kneeling down beside what was left of my fire, and scooping still more sand on to it.

Stella had stayed with him. I whistled for her. She came, but not at once. I could see she was reluctant to leave him. She was behaving very oddly. Stella Artois had never taken kindly to strangers, never. I felt disappointed in her, a bit betrayed, even.

When I next looked back, the fire was not smoking at all. It had been completely smothered, and the old man was nowhere to be seen.

For the rest of that day I stayed in my cave. For some reason I felt safe there. I suppose I had already begun to think of it as home. I had no other. I felt as an orphan must feel, abandoned and alone in the world. I was frightened, I was angry, I was completely bewildered.

I sat there trying to gather my thoughts. So far as I could tell – though I couldn't be sure of it – there were only the two of us on this island, the old man and me. In which case, it stood to reason that only he could have left me the fish and the bananas and the water. Surely that had been an act of kindness, a sign of friendship, of welcome? And yet, now, this same man had banished me to one end of the island as if I was a leper, and had made it quite clear that he never wanted us to meet ever again. And all because I had lit a fire? None of it made any sense at all, unless he was out of his head and completely mad.

I took a long hard look at my situation. I was

marooned on an island in the middle of nowhere, very probably with a madman for company, and a bunch of howling monkeys (at least one orang-utan amongst them) – and God knows what else might be hidden in the forest – and millions of mosquitoes that would eat me alive every night. I knew only one thing. I had to get away. But how? How was I ever going to get off the island unless I could attract the attention of some passing ship? I could be here for the rest of my life. The thought didn't bear dwelling on.

I wondered how long the old man had been on the island, and what might have brought him here in the first place. Who was he? And who was he, anyway, to tell me what I could and could not do? And why had he put out my fire?

I curled up in my cave, closed my eyes and just wished myself back home, or back on the *Peggy Sue* with my mother and father. Such wonderful dreaming almost lulled me to sleep, but the mosquitoes and the howling from the forest soon dragged me back to consciousness, to face once again all the appalling implications of my wretched predicament.

It came to me suddenly that I had seen the old

man's face somewhere before. I had no idea how that could be. As I lay there pondering this, I felt the piece of glass in my pocket pressing into my hip. My spirits were suddenly lifted. I still had my fireglass. I would build my fire again, but this time somewhere he wouldn't discover it. I would wait for a ship to come, and until then I would survive. The old man had survived in this place. If he could, I could. And I could do it alone too. I didn't need him.

I felt hungry again and thirsty, too. Tomorrow I would go into the forest and find food for myself. I would find water. Somehow or other I would catch fish too. I was good at fishing. If I could catch them in the reservoir back home and off the *Peggy Sue*, then I could catch them here.

I spent that night cursing the hordes of whirring insects that were homing in on me, and the chattering forest that would not be silent, that would not let me be. I kept seeing the reservoir in my mind's eye, and my mother laughing in her skipper's cap. I felt tears coming and tried not to think of her. I thought of the old man. I was still trying to remember what he had said his name was when I fell asleep.

I awoke and knew at once that he had been. It was as if I had dreamed it. Stella seemed to have dreamed the same dream for at once she was bounding up on to the rocks above the cave. She found what she clearly expected to be there – her bowl of water full again. And there, too, high on the shelf of rock beyond her, was the same upturned tin, my water bowl beside it, just as it had been the morning before. I knew it would be full, and I knew as I lifted aside the tin that the food would be there again.

As I sat there cross-legged on the rock, chewing ravenously on my fish and throwing pieces down for Stella to catch, I realised exactly what he meant to imply by this. We were not friends. We would not be friends. He would keep me alive, keep Stella alive, but only so long as I lived by his rules. I had to keep to my end of the island, and I must never light fires. It was all quite clear.

With any real hope of immediate rescue diminishing day by day, I became more and more resigned. I knew I had no choice but to accept his terms and go along with his regime, for the moment. He had now marked out a frontier, a boundary line in the sand from the forest down to the sea on both sides of the island – and he renewed it frequently, as often as it needed to be. Stella strayed over it of course – I couldn't prevent her – but I did not. It wasn't worth it. In spite of the animosity I had seen in his eyes and that huge knife in his belt, I didn't really think he would ever hurt me. But I was frightened by him, and because of that, and because I had too much to lose, I did not want to confront him. After all, he was providing us everyday with all the food and water we needed.

I was beginning to find some edible fruit for myself – in particular a prickly shelled fruit (rambutan, I later discovered). It was delicious, but I could never find enough and, besides, Stella would not eat it. I found the occasional coconut still intact, but often both the milk and flesh were foul. Once or twice I even tried climbing for them, but they were always too high and I very soon gave up.

I tried fishing in the shallows, fashioning a crude spear, a long stick I had sharpened on a rock, but I was always too slow in my strike. There was often plenty of fish but they were too small and too fast. So, like it or not, we still very much needed the daily ration of fish and fruit and water the old man was bringing us.

I had searched my end of the island for fresh water, but could find none. I thought often of trespassing into the old man's part of the forest to look for it, but I dared not. For the most part, I kept close to the forest tracks.

It wasn't only the old man's laws nor the howling of the monkeys – which I came to understand as a warning – that prevented me from venturing into his side of the island, it was the orang-utan, too. He had seemed placid enough, but I had no idea how he or his friends might react if they found me in their territory. I kept wondering too what other creatures might lurk unseen, waiting to ambush me in the dark damp of the forest. If the constant jungle talk was anything to go by, the place was crawling with all sorts of dreadful creatures.

Just the thought of the orang-utan and the terrors of the unknown in the forest were quite enough to deter me, enough to stifle both my curiosity and my courage. So I kept largely to my beach, my cave and the forest track up to my hilltop.

From high on my hill I did catch distant glimpses of

the old man. Often in the mornings I would see him spear-fishing in the shallows, sometimes alone, but often accompanied by a group of orang-utans, who sat on the beach and watched him, fourteen or fifteen of them I counted once. Occasionally he would be carrying one of the young ones on his back. When he moved amongst them, it seemed almost as if he was one of them.

Time and again I tried to stay awake until the old man came with the food at night, but I never managed it. I never even heard him, not once. But every morning the water would be there, the fish too (it often tasted smoky these days, which I liked better). The fruit would not always be the same. Much of it was strangely scented, and not at all to my liking. I ate it anyway. Besides bananas and coconut and berries, he would leave me breadfruit or jackfruit (at the time, of course, I had no idea what they were). I ate everything, but not so greedily now. I would try to save some of the fruit for an evening meal. But I could never bring myself to save the red bananas, they were just too delicious not to eat all at once.

My recurring nightmare was the mosquitoes at

night. From dusk onwards they searched me out, buzzed in on me and ate me alive. There was no hiding-place. My nights were one long torture, and in the morning I would scratch myself raw in places. Some of the bites, particularly on my legs, had now swelled up and become suppurating red sores. I found relief from them only by dunking myself often in the cool of the sea.

I tried sleeping in another cave, deeper and darker, but it smelled dreadful. Once I had discovered it was full of bats, I left at once. Wherever I slept the mosquitoes found me out soon enough. It got so that I dreaded the coming of every night. I cried out aloud in my misery as I swiped and flailed at them. I longed for the mornings, for the cool of the sea and the cool of the wind on my hilltop.

Here I would spend the greater part of my day, sitting on the very summit, looking out to sea and hoping, sometimes even praying too, for the sight of a ship. I would close my eyes tight shut and pray for as long as I could, and then open them again. Every time I did it, I really felt, really believed, there was a chance my prayers would be answered, that this time I would open my eyes and see the *Peggy Sue* sailing back to rescue me, but always the great wide ocean was empty, the line of the horizon quite uninterrupted. I was always disappointed of course, often dejected, but not yet completely despondent, not in those early weeks.

I had severe problems, too, with sunburn. I had learned rather late that I should keep all my clothes on all the time, and I made myself a hat to keep the sun off my face and my neck. It was very broad and Chinese-looking, made of palm leaves, the edges folded into one another. I was quite pleased with my handiwork.

Sunburn, I discovered, was a discomfort I could help to prevent, and that seawater could soothe. At noon I would go down the hill to shelter in my cave from the burning heat of the afternoon sun, and then afterwards I would go swimming. This was the moment Stella longed for each day. I spent long hours throwing a stick for her. She loved it and, to be truthful, so did I. It was the highlight of our day. We'd stop only when the darkness came down – it always came down surprisingly quickly too – and drove us back once more to our cave, back to my nightly battle with my bloodsucking tormentors.

One day, after yet another fruitless morning of watching on the hill, Stella and I were coming out of the forest when I spotted something lying on the sand just outside our cave. At a distance it looked like a piece of driftwood. Stella got there before me and was sniffing it over excitedly. I could see it now for what it was. It was not driftwood at all, but a roll of rush matting. I unrolled it. Inside, and neatly folded, was a sheet, a white sheet. He knew! The old man knew my miseries, my discomforts, my every need. He had been watching me all the time, and closely too. He must have seen me scratching myself, seen the red weals on my legs, on my arms, seen me sitting in the sea every morning to soothe away my sores. Surely this must mean that he had forgiven me now for lighting the fire?

I carried the matting inside the cave, unrolled it, wound myself in the sheet, and just lay there giggling with joy. I could pull the sheet right up over my face. Tonight there would be no way in for those cursed mosquitoes. Tonight they would go hungry.

I went racing along the beach to the boundary line where I stopped, cupped my hands to my mouth and shouted, 'Thank you! Thank you for my bed! Thank you! Thank you!' I didn't really expect an answer, and none came. I hoped he might come himself, but he didn't. So I wrote my thanks in the sand right by the boundary line and signed it. I wanted so much to see him again, to talk to him, to hear a human voice. Stella Artois had been a wonderful companion to me, good for confiding in, good for a cuddle, good for a game, but I so missed human company – my mother, my father, lost to me now, perhaps forever. I longed to see the old man, to speak to him, even if he was a bit mad, even if I couldn't understand much of what he was saying.

That night I was determined to stay awake for him but, comfortable on my new matting bed, protected and swaddled in my sheet, I went to sleep quickly and never woke once.

The next morning, after a breakfast of fish and jackfruit and coconut, Stella and I made our way back up to the top of my hill, or 'Watch Hill' as I now called it – the other one I had named 'His Hill'. I was repairing my Chinese hat, replacing some of the palm leaves – it never seemed to hold together for very long – when I looked up and saw a ship on the horizon. There was no mistake. It was the long bulky profile of a super-tanker.

Chapter 6

Abunai!

In an instant I was on my feet, shouting at the top of my voice and waving frantically. I leaped up and down screaming for them to stop, to hear me, to see me. 'I'm here! Here! I'm here!' Only when my throat was raw and I could shout no longer did I stop. The tanker crept tantalisingly slowly along the horizon.

It did not turn, and by then I knew it would not turn. I knew too that no one would be looking, and that even if they were, this entire island would be little more than a distant hazy hump on the horizon. How then could they possibly see me? I could only look on, helpless and distraught, as the tanker moved inexorably further and further away from me until it began to disappear over the horizon. This took all morning long, a morning of dreadful anguish.

As I stood watching on the summit of Watch Hill, my despair was replaced by a burning anger. If I had been allowed to have my fire, there would at least have been a chance they could have spotted the smoke. True, the old man had brought me a sleeping mat and a sheet. He was looking after me, he was keeping me alive, but he was also keeping me prisoner.

As the last vestige of the tanker sank from my view, I promised myself that I would never again let such a chance go by. I felt in my pocket. I still had my precious fire glass. I determined I would do it. I would build another fire, not down on the beach where he could find it, but up here on Watch Hill, behind the rocks and well out of his sight, even if he did have binoculars – and I now had to presume that he did. I would gather a great beacon of wood, but I would not light it. I would set it all up and wait until the moment I saw a ship. If this one had come, I reasoned, then another one would come, had to come, and when it did, I would have my fire glass ready, and a cache of paper-thin, tinder-dry leaves. I would make such a blazing inferno of a fire, a fire that would send up such a towering smoke signal that the next ship that happened along would have to see it.

So now I no longer spent my days just sitting on Watch Hill and waiting. Every hour I was up there I spent building my beacon. I would drag great branches up over the rocky scree from the forest below and pile them high, but on the seaward side of the hilltop – the perfect place for it to be seen by ships, when it was lit – but, in the meantime, not by the prying eyes of the old man who I thought of now as my captor. And he *would* be watching me – I was quite sure of that now. Through all the fetching and carrying, I kept well out of his sight. Only eyes from the sea could possibly have known what I was doing, and there were no eyes out there to see me.

It took several days of hard labour to build my secret beacon. I had almost finished when someone did indeed discover what I was up to, but it wasn't the old man.

I was heaving a massive branch on to the pile when I felt a sudden shadow come over me. An orang-utan was looking down at me from the rock above – I could not be sure it was the same one as before. He was on all fours, his great shoulders hunched, his head lowered, eyeing me slightly sideways. I dared not move. It was a stand-off, just as it had been before down on the beach.

He sat back and looked at me with mild interest for a while. Then he looked away, scratched his face nonchalantly and sloped off, stopping once to glance back at me over his shoulder before moving on into the shadow of the trees and away. It occurred to me as I watched him go that maybe he had been sent to spy on me, that he might go back and tell the old man what he had seen me doing. It was a ridiculous thought, I know, but I do remember thinking it.

A storm broke over the island that night, such a fearsome storm, such a thunderous crashing of lightning overhead, such a din of rain and wind that sleep was quite impossible. Great waves roared in from the ocean, pounding the beach, and shaking the ground beneath me. I spread out my sleeping mat at the very back of the cave. Stella lay down beside me and huddled close. How I welcomed that.

It was fully four days before the storm blew itself out, but even during the worst of it, I would find my fish and fruit breakfast waiting for me every morning under my tin, which he had now wedged tight in under the same shelf of rock. Stella and I kept to the shelter of our cave. All we could do was watch as the rain came lashing down outside. I looked on awestruck at the power of the vast waves rolling in from the open sea, curling, tumbling, and exploding as they broke on to the beach, as if they were trying to batter the island into pieces and then suck us all out to sea. I thought often of my mother and father and the *Peggy Sue*, and wondered where they were. I just hoped the typhoon – for that was what I was witnessing – had passed them by.

Then, one morning, as suddenly as the storm had begun, it stopped. The sun blazed down from a clear blue sky, and the forest symphony started up where it had left off. I ventured out. The whole island steamed and dripped. I went at once up Watch Hill to see if I could see a ship, perhaps blown off course, or maybe sheltering in the lee of the island. There was nothing there. That was a disappointment, but at least I found my beacon had not collapsed. It was sodden, of course, but still intact. Everything was sodden. There could be no fire now until it had dried out.

The air was hot and heavy all that day. It was difficult to move at all, difficult to breathe. Stella could only lie and pant. The only place to cool off was the sea, so I spent most of that day lolling lazily in the water, throwing the occasional stick for Stella to keep her happy.

I was lying in the sea, just floating there and day-dreaming, when I heard the old man's voice. He was hurrying down the beach, yelling at us as he came and waving his stick wildly in the air.

'*Yamero*! *Abunai*! Dangerous. Understand? No

swim.' He did not seem to be angry with me, as he had been before, but he was clearly upset about something.

I looked around me. The sea was still heaving in but gently now, breathing out the last of the storm, the waves falling limp and exhausted on to the beach. I could see no particular danger.

'Why not?' I called back. 'What's the matter?'

He had dropped his stick on the beach and was wading out through the surf towards me.

'No swim. *Dameda*! *Abunai*! No swim.' Then he had me by the arm and was leading me forcibly out of the sea. His grip was vice-like. There was little point in struggling. Only when we were back on the beach did he at last release me. He stood there breathless for a few moments. 'Dangerous. Very bad. *Abunai*!' He was pointing out to sea. 'No swim. Very bad. No swim. You understand?' He looked me hard in the eye, leaving me in no doubt that this was not meant as advice, this was a command that I should obey. Then he turned and walked off into the forest, retrieving his stick as he went. Stella ran after him, but I called her back.

I felt at that moment like defying him openly.

I would charge back into the sea and frolic as noisily, as provocatively as I could. That would show him. I was bristling at the outrageous unfairness of it all. First, he would not let me light my fire. Then I was banished to one end of the island, and now I wasn't even allowed to swim. I wanted to call him every name I could think of. But I didn't. I didn't go swimming in the sea again either. I capitulated. I gave in, because I had to. I needed his food, his water. Until my secret beacon of wood dried out, until the next ship came by, I would have to do as he said. I had no choice. I did make a mansize sculpture of him lying in the sand outside my cave, and I did jump up and down on him in my fury and frustration. It made me feel a little better, but not much.

Until now, except for occasional gut-wrenching pangs of homesickness and loneliness, I had by and large managed to keep my spirits up. But not any more. My beacon stayed obstinately damp. Everyday I went up Watch Hill hoping to sight a ship, and everyday the sea stretched away on all sides, empty. I felt more and more isolated, more and more wretched. In the end I decided not to go up onto Watch Hill any more, that it just was not worth it. Instead I stayed in my cave and curled up on my sleeping mat for long hours during the day. I lay there drowning in my misery, thinking of nothing but the hopelessness of it all, how I would never get off this island, how I would die here, and my mother and father would never even know what had happened to me. No one would, except the old man, the mad man, my captor, my persecutor.

The weather stayed heavy and humid. How I longed to plunge into the ocean, but I dared not. He'd be watching me for sure. With every day that passed, in spite of the fish and fruit and water he continued to bring me, I came to hate the old man more and more. Dejected and depressed I may have been, but I was angry too, and gradually this anger fuelled in me a new determination to escape, and this determination revived my spirits. Once again I went on my daily trek up Watch Hill. I began to collect a fresh cache of dry leaves and twigs from the forest edge and squirreled them away in a deep cleft in the rock so that I would always be sure they were dry, when the time came. My beacon had dried out at last. I built it up, higher and higher. When

I had done all I could I sat and waited for the time to come, as I knew it must. Day after day, week after week, I sat up on Watch Hill, my fire glass polished in my pocket, my beacon ready and waiting.

As it turned out, when the time did come, I wasn't up on Watch Hill at all. One morning, with sleep still in my head, I emerged from my cave, and there it was. A boat! A boat with strange red-brown sails – I supposed it to be some kind of Chinese junk – and not that far out to sea either. Excitement got the better of me. I ran helter-skelter down the beach, shouting and screaming for all I was worth. But I could see at once that it was hopeless. The junk was not that far out to sea, but it was still far too far for me to be either seen or heard. I tried to calm myself, tried to think . . . The fire! Light the fire!

I ran all the way up Watch Hill without once stopping, Stella hard on my heels and barking. All around me the forest was cackling and screeching and whooping in protest at this sudden disturbance. I readied my cache of dry leaves, took my fireglass and crouched down beside the beacon to light my fire. But I was trembling so much with excitement

and exhaustion by now that I could not hold my hand still enough. So I set up a frame of twigs and laid the glass over it, just as I had before. Then I sat over it, willing the leaves to smoulder.

Every time I looked out to sea the junk was still there, moving slowly away, but still there.

It seemed an age, but there was a wisp of smoke, and shortly afterwards a glorious, wondrous glow of flame spreading along the edge of one leaf. I bent over it to blow it into life.

That was when I saw his feet. I looked up. The old man was standing over me, his eyes full of rage and hurt. He said not a word, but set about stamping out my embryo fire. He snatched up my fireglass and hurled it at the rock below where it shattered to pieces. I could only look on and weep as he kicked away my precious pile of dry leaves, as he dismantled my beacon and hurled the sticks and branches one by one down the hill. As he did so the group of orang-utans gathered to watch.

Soon nothing whatsoever now remained of my beacon. All about me now the rocky scree was littered with the scattered ruins of it. I expected him to screech at me, but he didn't. He spoke very quietly, very deliberately. '*Dameda*,' he said.

'But why?' I cried. 'I want to go home. There's a boat, can't you see? I just want to go home, that's all. Why won't you let me? Why?'

He stood and stared at me. For a moment I thought I detected just a flicker of understanding. Then he bowed very stiffly from the waist, and said, '*Gomenasai. Gomenasai.* Sorry. Very sorry.' And with that he left me there and went off back into the forest, followed by the orang-utans.

I sat there watching the junk until it was nothing but a spot on the horizon, until I could not bear to watch any more. By this time I had already decided how I could best defy him. I was so enraged that consequences didn't matter to me now. Not any more. With Stella beside me I headed along the beach, stopped at the boundary line in the sand and then, very deliberately, I stepped over it. As I did so, I let him know precisely what I was doing.

'Are you watching, old man?' I shouted. 'Look! I've crossed over. I've crossed over your silly line. And now I'm going to swim. I don't care what you say. I don't care if you don't feed me. You hear me, old man?' Then I turned and charged down the beach into the sea. I swam furiously, until I was completely exhausted and a long way from the shore. I trod water and thrashed the sea in my fury – making it boil and froth all around me. 'It's my sea as much as yours,' I cried. 'And I'll swim in it when I like.'

I saw him then. He appeared suddenly at the edge of the forest. He was shouting something at me, waving his stick. That was the moment I felt it, a searing, stinging pain in the back of my neck, then my back, and my arms too. A large, translucent white jellyfish was floating right beside me, its tentacles groping at me. I tried to swim away but it came after me, hunting me. I was stung again, in my foot this time. The agony was immediate and excruciating. It permeated my entire body like one continuous electric shock. I felt my muscles going rigid. I kicked for the shore, but I could not do it. My legs seemed paralysed, my arms too. I was sinking, and there was nothing I could do about it. I saw the jellyfish poised for the kill above me now. I screamed, and my mouth filled with water. I was choking. I was going to die, I was going to drown but I did not care. I just wanted the pain to stop. Death I knew would stop it.

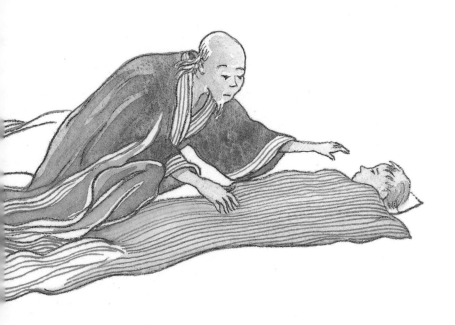

Chapter 7

All that silence said

I smelt vinegar, and thought I was at home. My father always brought us back fish and chips for supper on Fridays and he loved to soak his in vinegar — the whole house would stink of it all evening.

I opened my eyes. It was dark enough to be evening, but I was not at home. I was in a cave, but not my cave. I could smell smoke too. I was lying on a sleeping mat covered in a sheet up to my chin. I tried to sit up to look about me, but I could not move. I tried to turn my neck. I couldn't. I could move nothing except my eyes. I could feel though. My skin, my whole body throbbed with searing pain, as if I had been scalded all over. I tried to call out, but could barely manage a whisper. Then I remembered the jellyfish. I remembered it all.

The old man was bending over me, his hand soothing on my forehead. 'You better now,' he said. 'My name Kensuke. You better now.' I wanted to ask after Stella. She answered for herself by sticking her cold nose into my ear.

I do not know for how many days I lay there, drifting in and out of sleep, only that whenever I woke Kensuke was always there sitting beside me. He rarely spoke and I could not speak, but the silence between us said more than any words. My erstwhile enemy, my captor, had become my saviour. He would lift me to pour fruit juice or warm soup down my throat. He would sponge me down with cooling water, and when the pain was so bad that I cried out, he would hold me and sing me softly back to sleep. It was strange. When he sang to me it was like an echo from the past, of my father's voice perhaps – I didn't know. Slowly the pain left me. Tenderly he nursed me back to life. The day my fingers first moved was the very first time I ever saw him smile.

When at last I was able to turn my neck I would watch him as he came and went, as he busied himself about the cave. Stella would often come and lie beside me, her eyes following him too.

Every day now I was able to see more of where I was. In comparison with my cave down by the beach, this place was vast. Apart from the roof of vaulted rock above, you would scarcely have known it was a cave. There was nothing rudimentary about it at all. It looked more like an open plan house than a cave – kitchen, sitting-room, studio, bedroom, all in one space.

He cooked over a small fire which smoked continuously at the back of the cave, the smoke rising

through a small cleft high in the rocks above – a possible reason, I thought, why there were no mosquitoes to bother me. There always seemed to be something hanging from a wooden tripod over the fire, either a blackened pot or what looked like and smelled like long strips of smoked fish.

I could see the dark gleam of metal pots and pans lined up on a nearby wooden shelf. There were other shelves too lined with tins and jars, dozens of them of all sizes and shapes, and hanging beneath them innumerable bunches of dried herbs and flowers. These he would often be mixing or pounding, but I wasn't sure what for. Sometimes he would bring them over to me so that I could smell them.

The cave house was sparsely furnished. To one side of the cave mouth stood a low wooden table, barely a foot off the ground. Here he kept his paint- brushes, always neatly laid out, and several more jars and bottles, and saucers, too.

Kensuke lived and worked almost entirely near the mouth of the cave house where there was daylight. At nights he would roll out his sleeping mat across the cave from me, up against the far wall. I would wake in the early mornings sometimes and just watch him sleeping. He always lay on his back wrapped in his sheet and never moved a muscle.

Kensuke would spend many hours of every day kneeling at the table and painting. He painted on large shells but, much to my disappointment, he never showed me what he had done. Indeed, he rarely seemed pleased with his work, for just as soon as he had finished, he would usually wash off what he had done and start again.

On the far side of the cave mouth was a long work bench and, hanging up above it, an array of tools – saws, hammers, chisels, all sorts. And beyond the work bench were three large wooden chests in which he would frequently rummage around for a shell, perhaps, or a clean sheet. We had clean sheets every night.

Inside the cave he wore a wraparound dressing gown (a kimono, as I later knew it to be). He kept the cave house immaculately clean, sweeping it down once a day at least. There was a large bowl of water just inside the cave mouth. Every time he came in he would wash his feet and dry them before stepping inside.

The floor was entirely covered with mats made of

woven rushes, like our sleeping mats. And everywhere, all around the cave, to head height and above, the walls were lined with bamboo. It was simple, but it was a home. There was no clutter. Everything had its place and its purpose.

As I got better, Kensuke would go off, and leave me on my own more and more but, thankfully, never for too long. He'd return later, very often singing, with fish, perhaps fruit, coconuts or herbs, which he'd bring over to show me proudly. The orang-utans would sometimes come with him, but only as far as the cave mouth. They'd peer in at me, and at Stella, who always kept her distance from them. Only the young ones ever tried to venture in, and then Kensuke only had to clap at them and they'd soon go scooting off.

During those early days in the cave house I so much wished we could talk. There were a thousand mysteries, a thousand things I wanted to know. But it still hurt me to talk, and besides I felt he was quite happy with our silence, that he preferred it somehow. He seemed a very private person, and content to be that way.

Then one day, after hours of kneeling hunched over one of his paintings, he came over and gave it to me. It was a picture of a tree, a tree in blossom. His smile said everything. 'For you. Japan tree,' he said. 'I, Japanese person.' After that Kensuke showed me all the paintings he did, even the ones he later washed off. They were all in black and white wash, of orang-utans, gibbons, butterflies, dolphins and birds, and fruit. Only very occasionally did he keep one, storing it away carefully in one of his chests. He did keep several of the tree paintings, I noticed, always of a tree in blossom, a 'Japan tree', as he called it, and I could see he took particular joy in showing me these. It was clear he was allowing me to share something very dear to him. I felt honoured by that.

In the dying light of each day he would sit beside me and watch over me, the last of the evening sun on his face. I felt he was healing me with his eyes. At night, I thought often of my mother and my father. I so much wanted to see them again, to let them know I was still alive. But, strangely, I no longer missed them.

In time I found my voice again. The paralysis gradually lost its grip on me and my strength flowed back. Now I could go out with Kensuke, whenever he invited me, and he often did. To begin with, I would squat on the beach with Stella and watch him spear-fishing in the shallows. So still he stood, and his strike was lightning fast. Then one day he made me my own spear. I was to fish with him. He taught me where the bigger fish were, where the octopus hid under the rocks, how to stand still as a heron and wait, spear poised just above the water, my shadow falling behind me so that the fish were not frightened away. I tell you, spearing a fish for the first time was like scoring a winning goal for the Mudlarks back home – just about the best feeling in the world.

Kensuke seemed to know every tree in the forest, where all the fruit grew, what was ripe and what was not, what was worth climbing for. He climbed impossible trees nimbly, footsure and fearless. Nothing in the forest alarmed him, not the howling gibbons swinging above his head to drive him off their fruit, not the bees that swarmed about him when he carried down their comb from a hollow high in a tree (he used the honey for sugaring and bottling fruit). And always his family of orang-utans came along, shadowing us through the forest, patrolling the tracks ahead, scampering along behind. All Kensuke had to do was sing and they'd come.

They seemed almost hypnotised by the sound of his voice. They were intrigued by me and by Stella, but they were nervous and we were nervous, and for the time being we kept our distance from one another.

One evening, quite unexpectedly, as I was watching Kensuke at his fishing, one of the young ones clambered on to my lap and began to examine my nose with his finger, and then he investigated my ear. He pulled it rather harder than I liked, but I didn't yelp. After that the rest followed suit, using me as if I were a climbing-frame. Even the older ones, the bigger ones, would reach out and touch me from time to time, but thankfully they were always more reserved, more circumspect. But Stella still kept a certain distance from them, and they from her.

In all this time – I suppose I must have been some months on the island by now – Kensuke had said very little. The little English he did speak was clearly hard for him. When words were used between us they proved to be of little help in our understanding of each other. So we resorted for the most part to smiles and nods, to signing and pointing. Sometimes we even drew pictures in the sand to explain ourselves.

It was just about enough to get along. But there was so much that I was burning to find out. How had he come to be here all alone on the island? How long had he been here? And how had he come by all those pots and pans and tools, and the knife he always wore in his belt? How come one of his wooden chests was stuffed with sheets? Where had they come from? Where had he come from? And why was he being so kind to me now, so considerate, when he had clearly resented me so much before? But whenever I ventured any such question, he would simply shake his head and turn away from me like a deaf man ashamed of his affliction. I was never quite sure whether he really did not understand, or just did not *want* to understand. Either way I could see it made him uncomfortable, so I probed no more. Questions, it seemed, were an intrusion. I resigned myself to waiting.

Our life together was always busy, and regular as clockwork. Up at dawn and down the track a little way to bathe in the stream where it tumbled cold and fresh out of the hillside into a great cauldron of smooth rocks. We would wash our sheets and clothes here, too (he'd made me my own kimono by now), slapping and pounding them on the rocks, before hanging them out to dry on the branch of a nearby tree. Breakfast was a thick pulpy fruit juice which seemed different every day, and bananas or coconut. I never tired of bananas, but very soon became sick of coconut. The mornings were spent either fishing in the shallows or fruit gathering in the forest. Sometimes, after a storm, we scoured the beach for more of his painting shells – only the biggest and flattest would do – or for flotsam to join the stack of wood at the back of the cave. There were two stacks, one clearly for firewood, the other, I supposed, reserved for his woodwork. Then it was home to the cave house for a lunch of raw fish (always delicious) and usually breadfruit (always bland and difficult to swallow). A short nap after lunch for both of us and then he would settle down at his table to paint. As I watched I became so engrossed that the failing light of evening always came too soon for me. We would cook a fish soup over the fire. Everything went in, heads and tails, a dozen different herbs – Kensuke wasted nothing – and there were always red bananas afterwards, all I could eat. I never went hungry.

When supper was over we would sit together at the mouth of the cave and watch the last of the sun drop into the sea. Then, without a word, he'd stand up. We would bow solemnly to one another, and he would unroll his sleeping mat and leave me to mine.

To see Kensuke at his work was always a wonder to me – he was so intent, so concentrated in everything he did. But watching him paint was best of all. To begin with he would only let me kneel beside him and watch. I could sense that in this, too, he liked his privacy, that he did not want to be disturbed. On the table in front of him he put out three saucers: one saucer of octopus ink (for Kensuke, octopuses were not just for eating), one saucer of water and another for mixing. He always held his brush very upright and very steady in his hand, fingers down one side, thumb on the other. He would kneel bent over his work, his beard almost touching the shell he was painting – I think perhaps he was a little short-sighted. I would watch him for hours on end, marvelling at the delicacy of his work, at the sureness of his touch.

Then one rainy afternoon – and when it rained,

how it rained – I found he'd set out a shell for me, my own three saucers and my own paint-brush. He took such a delight in teaching me, in my every clumsy attempt. I remember early on I tried to paint the jellyfish that had attacked me. He laughed out loud at that, but not in a mocking way, rather in recognition, in memory, of what had brought us together. I had always liked to draw, but from Kensuke I learned to love it, that to draw or paint I first had to observe well, then set out the form of the picture in my head and send it down my arm through the tip of the brush and on to the shell. He taught me all this entirely without speaking. He simply showed me.

The evidence that he was a considerable craftsman was all around me. The cave house must have been entirely furnished by him, fashioned mostly from flotsam: the chests, the workbench itself, the shelves, the table. He must have made the rush matting, the bamboo panelling, everything. And on close examination I could see it was all perfectly finished, no nails, no screws, just neat dowelling. He had used some form of glue where necessary, and sometimes twine as well. Ropes for tree-climbing, fishing-spears, fishing-nets and fishing-rods were stacked in one corner (though I'd never yet seen him use the rods). He had to have made them all.

He'd made his own paint-brushes as well, and I was soon to find out how. Kensuke had a favourite orang-utan, a large female he called Tomodachi, who would often come and sit by him to be groomed. Kensuke was grooming her one day just outside the mouth of the cave house, the other orang-utans looking on, when I saw him quite deliberately pluck out the longest and darkest hairs from her back. He held them up to show me, grinning conspiratorially. At the time I didn't really understand what he was up to. Later, I watched him at his work bench trimming the hairs with his knife, dipping them in the sap I'd seen him tap from a tree that same morning, cutting out a short length of hollow bamboo and then filling it with Tomodachi's hair. A day later the glue had hardened and he had a paint-brush. Kensuke seemed to have found ways to satisfy his every need.

We were silent at our painting one day, the rain thundering down on the forest below, when he stopped, put down his paint-brush, and said very slowly, in a very measured way, as if he'd thought about how to say it for a long time, 'I teach you painting, Mica.' (This was the first time he had ever called me by my name.) 'You teach me speak English. I want speak English. You teach me.'

It was the beginning of an English lesson that was to last for months. Every day, dawn to dusk, I translated the world around him into English. We did what we had always done, but now I talked all the while and he would echo every word, every phrase he wanted to. His brow would furrow with the effort of it.

It was as if by saying each word he simply swallowed it into his brain. Once told, once practised, he would rarely forget, and if he did, he was always very annoyed with himself. Sometimes as I enunciated a new word, I noticed that his eyes would light up. He would be nodding and smiling almost as if he recognised the word, as if he was greeting an old friend. He would repeat it again and again, savouring the sound of it before committing it to memory for good. And, of course, the more words he knew, the more he tried to experiment with them. Single words became clipped phrases, became entire sentences. His pronunciation, though, never did improve, however hard he tried. Michael was always Mica – sometimes Micasan. Now at last we could talk more easily to one another, the long silence in which our friendship had been forged was over. It had never been a barrier between us, but it had been limiting.

We were sitting by the cave mouth one sunset, when he said, 'You see now if I understand, Micasan. You tell me story, story of you, where you live, why you come here my island. From baby to now. I listen.'

So I did. I told him about home, about my mother and father, about the brick factory closing, about football with Eddie and the Mudlarks, about the *Peggy Sue* and our voyage round the world, about football in Brazil and lions in Africa and spiders in Australia, about my mother being ill, about the night I fell overboard.

'Very good. I understand. Very good,' he said when I had finished. 'So, football you like. When I little, I play football too. Very happy time, long ago now, in Japan, in my home.' He sat in silence for some moments. 'You very long way from home, Micasan. You very sad sometimes. I see. So, I make you happy. Tomorrow we go fishing and maybe I tell you my story too. My story, your story, maybe same story now.' The sun had suddenly gone. We stood up and bowed to one another. '*Oyasumi masai*', he said.

'Good night,' I said. It was the only time of the day he ever spoke Japanese, though he did sing in Japanese – mostly. I had taught him 'Ten Green Bottles', which always made him laugh when he sang it. I loved his laugh. It was never loud, more a prolonged chuckle; but it always warmed my heart.

The next morning, he picked up two of his fishing-rods and a net, and led the way into the forest. 'Today we catch big fish, Mica, not small fish,' he announced. He was taking us to the part of the island where I had been washed up all those months before, but rarely had cause to visit since, because there was little or no fruit to be found there. We had to beat a difficult path through the forest before joining a cliff path that wound its way down to a hidden sandy bay. As we emerged from the forest on to the beach, Stella ran off, bounding at once into the shallows, barking at me to play with her.

Suddenly, Kensuke caught me by the arm. 'You look, Micasan. What you see?' His eyes were full of mischief. I didn't know what I was supposed to be looking for. 'Nothing here, yes? I very clever fellow. You watch. I show you.' He made for the end of the beach, and I followed. Once there he began to pull and tug at the undergrowth. To my surprise it simply came away in his hands. I saw first what looked like a log lying in the sand but then, as he dragged away more branches, I saw it was part of a boat, an outrigger, a long wide dugout with a frame of outriggers on either side. It was covered in canvas which he folded back very slowly, chuckling to himself as he did so.

And there lying in the bottom of the boat beside a long oar was my football. He reached in and tossed it to me. It was softer now and much of the white leather was cracked and discoloured, but in places I could still just make out Eddie's name.

Chapter 8
Everyone dead in Nagasaki

I was overjoyed. I had found a part of me that I thought I had lost for ever. 'Now,' Kensuke said, beaming at me. 'Now you happy person, Micasan. I happy too. We go fishing. I tell you very soon where

I find this ball. Very soon I tell you everything. Little fish not so good now. Not so many. We need big fish sometimes from deep sea. We smoke fish. Then we have always plenty fish to eat. You understand?'

The outrigger was a great deal heavier than it looked. I helped Kensuke drag it down the beach and into the sea. 'This very good boat,' he said, as we lifted Stella in. 'This boat never go down. I make myself. Very safe boat.' He pushed us off and jumped in. I never ceased to be amazed at his extraordinary agility and strength. He rowed with a single oar, standing in the stern of the boat, more as if he was punting. Very soon we were out beyond the shelter of the cave and into the swell of the open sea.

Clutching my beloved football, and with Stella at my feet, I sat watching him and waiting for him to begin his story. I knew better than to pester him by now. The fishing came first. We baited our lines and settled silently to our fishing, one over each side of the boat. I was bursting to ask him about the football, about how he'd found it, but I dared not, for fear he would clam up and say nothing. It was some time before he began, but when he did it was well worth waiting for.

'Now I tell you everything, Micasan' he said, 'like I promise. I am old, but it is not long story. I am born in Japan, in Nagasaki. Very big town, by the sea. I grow up in this town. When I young man I study medicine in Tokyo. Soon I am Doctor, Doctor Kensuke Ogawa. I very proud person. I look after many mothers, many babies too. I first person many babies see in world. Then I go to London. I do studies in London, Guy's Hospital. You know this place?' I shook my head. 'Of course I learn speak little English there. Afterwards I came back to Nagasaki. I have beautiful wife, Kimi. Then I have little son too, Michiya. I very happy person in those days. But soon war comes. All Japanese men are soldiers now, sailors maybe. I go to navy. I doctor on big warship.'

A fish tugged on his line and took his bait, but not the hook. He went on as he rebaited his hook. 'This war very long time ago now.' I did know something of a war with Japan – I had seen it on films – but I knew very little about it. He shook his head. 'Many die in this war. This war very terrible time. Many ships go down. Japanese army win many battles. Japanese navy win many battles. All Japanese very happy people. Like football, when you win you happy. When you lose, you sad. I go home often, I see my Kimi and my little Michiya in Nagasaki. He grow fast. Already big boy. We all very happy family.'

'But war go on long time. Many Americans come, many ships, many planes, many bombs. Now war is not so good for Japan. We fight, but now we lose. Very bad time. We are in big sea battle. American planes come. My ship is bombed. There is fire and smoke. Black smoke. Many men burned. Many men dead. Many jump off ship into sea. But I stay. I am doctor, I stay with my patients. Planes come again. Many more bombs. I think I am dead person this time for sure. But I am not. I look all round ship. All patients dead. All sailors dead. I am only person alive on ship, but engine is still going. Ship moving on her own. She go now where she want to go. I cannot turn wheel. I can do nothing. But I listen to radio. Americans say on radio, big bomb fall on Nagasaki, atomic bomb. Many dead.

I very sad person. I think Kimi dead, Michiya dead. My mother live there too, all my family. I think they all dead.

'Soon radio say Japan surrender. I so sad I want to die.' He fished in silence for a while before he began again. 'Soon engine stop, but ship not go down. Big wind come, big storm. I think I die for sure now. But sea take ship and bring me here on this island. Ship come on to beach, and still I am not dead.'

'Very soon I find food. I find water also. I live like beggar man for long while. Inside I feel bad person. I think, all my friends dead, all my family dead, and I alive. I not want to live. But soon I meet orang-utans. They very kind to me. This very beautiful, very peaceful place. No war here, no bad people. I say to myself, Kensuke, you very lucky person to be alive. Maybe you stay here.

'I take many things from ship, I take food, I take clothes, sheets. I take pots. I take bottles. I take knife. I take binoculars. I take medicine. I find many things, many tools also. I take everything I find. When Kensuke finish, not much left on ship, I tell you. I find cave. I hide all things in cave. Soon terrible storm come, and ship go on rocks. Very soon she go down.

'One day American soldiers come. I hide. I not want to surrender, not honourable thing to do. I very afraid too. I hide in forest with orang-utans. Americans make fire on beach. They laugh in the night. I listen. I hear them. They say everyone dead in Nagasaki. They very happy about this. They laugh. I very sure now I stay on this island. Why go home? Soon Americans, they go away. My ship under water by now. They not find it. My ship still here. Under sand now, part of island now.'

The rusting hull I had found that first day on the island! So much was beginning to make sense to me now. A fish took my line suddenly, almost jerking the rod from my grasp. Kensuke leaned across to help me. It took many minutes of heaving to bring the fish to the surface, but between us we managed to haul it in. We sat back exhausted as it floundered at the bottom of the boat at our feet. It was massive, bigger even that the biggest fish I'd ever seen, the pike my father had caught in the reservoir back home. Kensuke dispatched it quickly, a sharp blow to the back of the neck with the handle of his knife. 'Good fish. Very good fish. You very clever fisherman person, Mica. We good together. Maybe we catch more now.'

But it was many hours before we caught another, though it did not seem like it. Kensuke told me of his life alone on the island, how he had learned to survive, to live off the land. He learned he said mostly by watching what the orang-utans ate, and what they did not eat. He learned to climb as they did. He learned to understand their language, to heed their warning signals – the darting eyes, the nervous scratching. Slowly he built a bond of trust and became one of them.

By the time we made for home that evening with three huge fish in the bottom of the boat – tuna I think they were – his story was almost finished. He talked on as he rowed. 'After Americans, no more men come to my island. I alone here many years. I not forget Kimi. I not forget Michiya. But I live. Then year ago, maybe, they come. Very bad people, killer men. They have guns. They hunt.

They shoot. I sing to my orang-utans. They come to me when I sing. They are very frightened. They come all in my cave. We hide. Killer men not find us. But in forest they shoot – you told me name – gibbon monkeys. They shoot mothers. They take babies. Why must they do this? I very angry. I think, all people killer people. I hate all people, I think. I not want see people again.

'Then one day I need big fish to smoke, I go fishing in this boat. Wind blow wrong way. I go far out. Sea pull me away very strong. I try to come back my island. It is no good. I am old. Arms are not strong. When night come I am still far away. I very frightened. I sing. It make me brave. I hear shout. I see light. I think I dream. Then I hear another song in sea, in dark. I come quick as I can. I find you and Stella and ball. You very nearly dead person, Micasan. Stella very nearly dead dog.' So it had been Kensuke who had pulled me from the sea, Kensuke who had saved me. It had simply never occurred to me.

'In morning,' he went on, 'sea bring us again near my island. I very glad you not dead. But I very angry person too. I want to be alone. I not want to see people. For me all people killer people. I not want you on my island. I carry you. I leave you on beach. I leave you food. I leave you water so you not die. But you make fire. I want people stay away. I not want people find me here on my island. Maybe they come. Maybe they shoot orang-utan, shoot gibbon monkey. Maybe they find me, take me away too. I very angry person, I put out fire. I not want speak to you. I not want see you. I draw line in sand.

'Big storm come, biggest I ever see. After storm, sea full of white jellyfish. I know these jellyfish. Very bad. They touch you, you very dead. I know this. I say, do not swim, very dangerous. Very soon I see you make big fire on top of hill. I think you very wicked person. I very angry now, and you very angry too. You swim in sea. Jellyfish sting. I think for sure you dead person. But you very strong. You live. I bring you into cave. I have vinegar. I make from berries. Vinegar kill poison. You live, Mica, but for long time you very sick boy. You strong again, and we friends now. We very good friends.'

So that was it, the whole story. He stopped rowing for a while, and smiled down at me. 'You are like son to me now. We happy people. We paint. We fish. We happy. We stay together. You my family now, Micasan. Yes?'

'Yes,' I said. I meant it and felt it too.

He let me take the oar, and showed me how to row his way, standing up, feet planted well apart. It wasn't as easy as he made it look. Clearly he trusted me to get us back, for he sat back in the bow of the outrigger to rest and fell asleep almost at once, his mouth open, his face sunken. He always looked even older when he slept. As I watched him I tried to picture his face as it must have been when he first came to the island all those years ago, over forty years. I owed him so very much. He had saved my life twice, fed me and befriended me. He was right. We were happy, and I was his family.

But I had another family too. I thought of the last time I had been out in a boat, of my mother and my father and how they must be grieving for me every day, every night. By now they must surely believe I was drowned, that there was no chance I could be alive. But I *wasn't* drowned. I *was* alive. Somehow I had to let them know it. As I struggled to bring the outrigger back to the island that afternoon, I was filled with a sudden powerful longing to see them again, to be with them. I could steal the boat I thought. I could row away, I could light a fire again. But I knew even as I thought it that I could not do it. How could I ever leave Kensuke now, after all he had done for me? How could I betray his trust? I tried to put the whole idea out of my mind, and I really believe I would have too. But the very next morning, I found the plastic Coke bottle washed up on the beach, and after that the idea of escape came back and haunted me day and night, and would not leave me be.

For some days, I kept the Coke bottle buried under the sand, whilst I wrestled with my conscience or, rather, justified what I wanted to do. It wouldn't really be a betrayal, not as such, I told myself. Even if the bottle was found no one would know where to come to, they'd just know I was alive. I made up my mind I would do it, and do it as soon as I could.

Kensuke had gone off octopus fishing. I had stayed behind to finish a shell painting – or so I had told him. I found an old sheet at the bottom of one of his chests and tore away a small corner of it. Then I knelt down at the table, stretched it out and painted my message on it in octopus ink:

To: the *Peggy Sue*. Fareham. England.
Dear Mum and Dad,
I am alive. I am well. I live on an island.
I do not know where. Come and find me.
    Love,
    Michael

I waited until it was dry, then I rolled it up, dug my Coke bottle out of the sand, slipped in my message and screwed the bottle up tight. I made quite sure Kensuke was still intent on his fishing, and set off.

I ran the entire length of the island keeping always to the forest, so that there was no chance Kensuke could see where I was going or what I was up to. The gibbons howled their accusations at me all the way, the entire forest cackling and screeching its condemnation. I just hoped Stella would not bark back at them, would not betray where I was. Fortunately she didn't.

At last I reached the rocks under Watch Hill. I leaped from rock to rock until I was standing right at the very end of the island, the waves washing over my feet. I looked round me. Stella was the only witness. I hurled the bottle as far out to sea as I possibly could. Then I stood and watched it as it bobbed away and out to sea. It was on its way.

I didn't touch my fish soup that night. Kensuke thought I was ill. I could hardly talk to him. I couldn't look him in the eye. I lay all night in deep torment, racked by my guilt, yet at the same time still hoping against hope that my bottle would be picked up.

Kensuke and I were at our painting the next afternoon when Stella came padding into the cave. She had the Coke bottle in her mouth. She dropped it and looked up at me, panting and pleased with herself.

Kensuke laughed and reached down to pick it up. I think he was about to hand it to me when he noticed there was something inside it. By the way he looked at me I was quite sure he knew at once what it was.

Chapter 9

The night
of the turtles

There fell between us a long and aching silence. Kensuke never once reproached me for what I had done. He was not angry or sullen at me. But I knew I had hurt him to the soul. It wasn't that we didn't speak

– we did – but we no longer talked to one another as we had before. We lived each of us in our separate cocoons, quite civil, always polite, but not together any more. He had closed in on himself and wrapped himself in his thoughts. The warmth had gone from his eyes, the laughter in the cave house was silenced. He never said so – he did not need to – but I knew that now he would prefer to paint alone, to fish alone, to be alone.

So, day after day, I wandered the island with Stella, hoping when I returned that he might have forgiven me, that we could be friends again. But always he kept that distance between us. I grieved for my lost friendship. I remember I went often now to the other end of the island, to Watch Hill, and sat there and sat there, no longer looking out for ships, but rehearsing aloud my explanation. But no matter how much I rehearsed it, how I reasoned it, I could never convince even myself that what I had done was anything other than treachery. In the end, as it turned out, it was Kensuke who explained it to me.

We had just gone to bed one night when Tomodachi came to the mouth of the cave and squatted there. She had done this once or twice lately, stayed for just a few minutes, peered in at us and gone off again. Kensuke spoke up in the darkness. 'She lose Kikanbo again,' he said. 'She always lose her baby. Kikanbo very wicked baby. He run off a lot. He make Tomodachi very sad mother.' He clapped his hands at her, shooing her away. 'Kikanbo not here, Tomodachi. Not here.' But Tomodachi stayed, I think for comfort more than anything else. I had noticed before with the orang-utans, how they would often come to Kensuke when they were upset or frightened, just to be near him. After a while Tomodachi slunk off into the night and left us alone again, with the din of the forest and the silence between us.

'I think many thoughts,' Kensuke said suddenly, out of the silence. 'You are sleeping, Micasan?' He had not called me by my name for weeks, ever since the Coke bottle incident.

'No,' I said.

'Very good. I got lot to say. You listen. I talk. I think many thoughts. When I think of Tomodachi, I think of your mother. Your mother, she too lose her baby. She lose you. That very sad thing for her.

Maybe she come looking, and she not find you. You not there when she come. She think you dead for ever. But she see you in her mind. Now as I speak maybe she see you in her mind. You always there. I know. I have son too. I have Michiya. He always in my head. Like Kimi. They dead for sure, but they in my head. They in my head forever.'

For a long while he did not say another word. I thought he had gone to sleep. Then he spoke again. 'I tell you everything I think, Micasan. It best way. I stay on this island because I want stay on this island. I do not want go home Japan. Different thing for you. You want go back home across the sea, and that right thing, good thing for you. But not good for me. For me, very sad thing. Many years I live alone here. I happy here. Then you come. I hate you when you first come. But after little while you are like son to me. I think maybe I like father to you, you like son to me. I very sad now when you go. I like talk with you. I like listen. I like sound when you speak. I want you stay here on this island. You understand?'

'I think so,' I said.

'But you do one very bad thing. We friends, but

you not tell me what you feel. You not say what you do. That not honourable thing to do. When I find bottle, when I read words, I very sad person indeed. But after little while I understand. I think maybe you want stay here with me, and you want also go home. So when you find bottle, you write message. You do not say what you do because you know it make me sad. I right, yes?'

'Yes,' I said.

'You very young person, Micasan. You paint good picture, very good picture, like Hokusai. You have long life waiting for you. You cannot live whole life on this island with old man who die one day. So, thinking like this, I change my mind. You know what we do tomorrow?' He didn't wait for me to answer. 'We start build new fire, big fire. We ready then for when we see ship. Then you go home. And also we do another thing. We play football, you, me. What you say?'

'All right.' It was all I could say. He had in just those few moments lifted the whole weight of guilt off my shoulders and given me such happiness, such new hope.

'Very good. Very good. You sleep now. We do lot
of work tomorrow, lot of football also.'

The next morning we began building a beacon on
the hilltop above the cave house. We used most of the
pile of firewood we had collected for the cooking fire
and stored in the dry at the back of the cave – he even
sacrificed some of his best pieces of driftwood. It
wasn't far to carry it, so before long we had enough to

make a sizeable fire. Kensuke said it would do for the moment, that we could find more from the forest, more and more each day as we wanted. 'We soon have fire so big they see in Japan maybe,' he laughed. 'We have lunch now, then sleep, then football. Yes?'

Later that afternoon we set up sticks in the sand for a goal and took turns at shooting at each other. The ball was very soft, and so it didn't bounce any better on the sand than it had back on the mud of the recreation ground back home, but it didn't matter. Kensuke may have carried a stick, he may have been as old as the hills, but he could kick a football well enough to put it past me, and often too.

What a time we had. Neither of us wanted it to end. With a crowd of bemused orang-utans looking on, with Stella interfering and chasing after every goal scored, we were at it till darkness drove us at last back up the hill. We were both too tired to do more than have a long drink of water, eat a banana or two and go to our sleeping mats.

It was after our reconciliation that I came to know Kensuke better than I ever had before. His English became more and more fluent, and he clearly loved to speak it now. For some reason he was always more happy to talk while we were out fishing in his outrigger. We did not go out that often, only when the fishing was so poor in the shallows that we needed to catch big fish for smoking and keeping.

Once at sea, the stories simply flowed. He talked a great deal of his childhood in Japan, of his twin sister and how the worst thing he'd ever done was to push her out of the tree in their garden, how she'd broken her arm, how when he painted that cherry tree it always reminded him of her. But she too had been in Nagasaki when the bomb fell. I remember he even told me the address of where he lived when he was studying in London – No. 22 Clanricarde Gardens, I have never forgotten it. Once he had gone to watch Chelsea playing football and afterwards he'd sat astride a lion in Trafalgar Square and been ticked off by a policeman.

But it was Kimi and Michiya he talked of most, about how he wished he could have seen Michiya grow up. Michiya, he said, would have been nearly fifty by now if the bomb hadn't fallen on Nagasaki, and Kimi would be exactly the same age as he was, seventy-five. I rarely interrupted him when he was like this, but once to comfort him I did say, 'Bombs don't kill everyone. They could still be alive. You never know. You could find out. You could go home.' He looked at me then as if it was the first time such a possibility had ever occurred to him in all those years. 'Why not?' I went on. 'When we see a ship and we light the fire and they come and fetch me, you could come too. You could go back to Japan. You don't have to stay here.'

He thought about it for some time, but then shook his head. 'No,' he said. 'They are dead. That bomb was very big bomb, very terrible bomb. Americans say Nagasaki is destroyed, every house. I hear them. My family dead for sure. I stay here. I safe here. I stay on my island.'

Day after day we piled more and more wood on the beacon. It was massive now, bigger even than the one I had built on Watch Hill. Every morning now before we went down to the pool to wash, Kensuke would send me up to the top of the hill with his binoculars. I always scanned the horizon both in hope and in trepidation. I longed to see a ship, of course I did. I longed to go home. But at the same time I dreaded what that would mean. I felt so much at home with Kensuke. The thought of leaving him filled me with a terrible sadness. I determined to do all I could to persuade him to come away with me, if and when a ship came.

At every opportunity now I talked to him of the

outside world, and the more I talked the more he seemed to become interested. Of course, I never spoke of the wars and famines and disasters. I painted the best picture of the world outside I could. There was so much he didn't know. He marvelled at all I told him, at the microwave in our kitchen, at computers and what they could do, at Concorde flying faster than the speed of sound, at men going to the moon, and satellites. These things took some explaining, I can tell you. Some of it he didn't even believe, not at first.

The time came when he began to quiz me. In particular he would ask about Japan. But I knew very little about Japan, only that back home in England lots of things, including our microwave, had 'made in Japan' written on them: cars, calculators, my father's stereo, my mother's hair dryer.

'I "made in Japan" person,' he laughed. 'Very old machine, still good, still very strong.'

Try as I did to trawl my memory, after a while I could find nothing more to tell him about Japan, but he would still keep asking. 'You sure there no war in Japan these days?' I was fairly certain there wasn't and said so. 'They build up Nagasaki again after bomb?' I told him they had, and hoped I was right. All I could do was to reassure him as best I could, and then tell him the same few things I did know about over and over again. He seemed to love to hear it, like a child listening to a favourite fairy story.

Once, after I'd finished expounding yet again on the amazing sound quality of my father's brilliant Sony stereo that made the whole house vibrate, he said very quietly, 'Maybe one day before I die I go back to my home. One day I go back to Japan. Maybe.' I wasn't sure he meant it, but it did mean that he was at least considering it, and that gave me some cause for hope. It wasn't until the night of the turtles though, that I came to believe Kensuke was really serious about it.

I was fast asleep when he woke me. 'You come, Micasan. Very quickly you come. You come,' he said.

'What for?' I asked him, but he was already gone. I ran out after him into the moonlight and caught him up halfway down the track. 'What are we doing. Where are we going? Is it a boat?'

'Very soon you see. Very soon.' Stella stayed at my heels all the way to the beach. She never liked going out in the dark very much. I looked around. There was nothing there. The beach looked completely deserted. The waves lapped listlessly. The moon rode the clouds, and the world felt still about me as if it was holding its breath. I did not see what was happening until Kensuke suddenly fell on his knees in the sand. 'They very small. Sometimes they are not so strong. Sometimes in the morning birds come and eat them.' And then I saw it.

I thought it was a crab at first. It wasn't. It was a minuscule turtle, tinier than a terrapin, clambering out of a hole in the sand and then beetling off down the beach towards the sea. Then another, and another, and further down the beach dozens of them, hundreds I could see now, maybe thousands, all scuttling across the moonlit sand into the sea. Everywhere the beach was alive with them. Stella was nosing at one, so I warned her off. She yawned and looked innocently up at the moon.

I saw that one of them was on its back at the bottom of the hole, legs kicking frantically. Kensuke reached down, picked it up gently and set it on its feet in the sand. 'You go to sea, little turtle,' he said. 'You live there now. You soon be big fine turtle, and then one day you come back and see me maybe.' He sat back on his haunches to watch him scuttle off. 'You know what they do, Mica. Mother turtles, they lay eggs in this place. Then, one night-time every year, always when moon is high, little turtles are born. Long way to go to sea. Very many die. So always I stay. I help them. I chase birds away, so they not eat baby turtles. Many years from now, when turtles are big, they come back. They lay eggs again. True story, Micasan.'

All night long we kept our vigil over the mass birth, as the infant turtles made their run for it. We patrolled together, reaching into every hole we found to see if there were any left, stuck or stranded. We found several too weak to make the journey, and carried them down into the sea ourselves. The sea seemed to revive them. Away they went, no swimming lessons needed. We turned dozens the right way up and shepherded them safely into the sea.

When dawn came and the birds came down to scavenge, we were there to drive them off. Stella chased and barked after them, and we ran at them, shrieking, waving, hurling stones. We were not entirely successful, but most of the turtles made it down into the sea. But even here they were still not entirely safe. In spite of all our desperate efforts a few were plucked up out of the water by the birds and carried off.

By noon it was all over. Kensuke was tired as we stood ankle deep in the water watching the very last of them swim away. He put his arm on my shoulder. 'They very small turtles, Micasan, but they very brave. They braver than me. They do not know what they find out there, what happen to them; but they go anyway. Very brave. Maybe they teach me good lesson. I make up my mind. When one day ship come, and we light fire, and they find us, then I go. Like turtles I go. I go with you. I go home to Japan. Maybe I find Kimi. Maybe I find Michiya. I find truth. I go with you, Micasan.'

Chapter 10

Killer men come

Shortly after this the rains came and forced us to shelter for days on end inside the cave house. The tracks became torrents, the forest became a swamp. I longed for the howl of the gibbons instead of the roar of the rain on the trees outside. It did not rain in fits and starts as it did at home, but constantly, incessantly. I worried over our beacon, that was becoming more saturated now with every passing day. Would it ever dry out? Would this rain ever stop? But Kensuke was stoical about it all. 'It stop when it stop, Micasan,' he told me. 'You cannot make rain stop by wanting it to stop. Besides, rain very good thing. Keep fruit growing. Keep stream flowing. Keep monkeys alive, you also, me also.'

I did make a dash up to the hilltop each morning with the binoculars, but I don't know why I bothered. Sometimes it was raining so hard I could hardly see the sea at all.

Occasionally we sallied out into the forest to gather enough fruit to keep us going. There were berries growing in abundance now, which Kensuke insisted on gathering – he didn't seem to mind getting soaked to the skin as much as I did. We ate some, but most he turned into vinegar. The rest he bottled in honey and water. 'For rainy day, yes?' he laughed. (He loved experimenting with the new expressions he had picked up.) We ate a lot of smoked fish – he always seemed to have enough in reserve. It made me very thirsty, but I never tired of it.

I remember the rainy season more for the painting we did than for anything else. We painted together for hours on end – until the octopus ink ran out. These days Kensuke was painting more from his memory – his house in Nagasaki, and several portraits of Kimi and Michiya standing together, always under the cherry tree. The faces, I noticed, he always left very indistinct. He once explained this to me. (He was more and more fluent now in his English.)

'I remember who they are,' he said. 'I remember where they are. I can hear them in my head, but I cannot see them.'

I spent days perfecting my first attempt at an orang-utan. It was of Tomodachi. She would often crouch soulful and dripping at the cave mouth, almost as if she was posing for me. So I took full advantage.

Kensuke was ecstatic in his delight at my painting, and lavish in his praise. 'One day, Micasan, you will be fine painter, like Hokusai, maybe.' That was the first shell painting of mine he kept and stored away in his chest. I felt so proud. After that he insisted on keeping many of my shell paintings. He would often take them out of the chest and study them carefully, showing me where I might improve, but always generously. Under his watchful eye, in the glow of his encouragement, every picture I painted seemed more accomplished, more how I wanted it to be.

Then one morning the gibbons were howling again and the rains had stopped. We went fishing in the shallows, out at sea too, and had very soon replenished our stores of smoked fish and octopus ink. We played football again. And all the while the beacon on the hilltop was drying out.

Wherever we went now we took the binoculars with us, just in case. We very nearly lost them once when Kikanbo, Tomodachi's errant son – always the cheekiest, most playful of all the young orang-utans stole them and ran off into the forest. When we caught up with him he didn't want to surrender them at all. In the end Kensuke had to bribe him – a red banana for a pair of binoculars.

But as time passed we were beginning to live as if

we were going to be staying on the island for ever, and that began to trouble me deeply. Kensuke made repairs to his outrigger. He made more vinegar. He collected herbs and dried them in the sun. And he seemed less and less interested in looking for a ship. He seemed to have forgotten all about it.

He sensed my restlessness. He was working on the boat one day and, ever hopeful, I was scanning the sea through the binoculars. 'It is easier when you are old like me, Micason,' he said.

'What is?' I asked.

'Waiting,' he said. 'One day a ship will come, Micasan. Maybe soon, maybe not so soon. But it will come. Life must not be spent always hoping, always waiting. Life is for living.' I knew he was right, of course, but only when I was lost and absorbed in my painting was I truly able to obliterate all thoughts of rescue, all thoughts of my mother and father.

I woke one morning and Stella was barking outside the cave house. I got up and went out after her. At first she was nowhere to be seen. When I did find her, she was high up on the hill, half growling, half barking, and her hackles were up. I soon saw why. A junk! A small junk far out to sea. I scrambled down the hill and met Kensuke coming out of the cave house buckling his belt. 'There's a boat!' I cried. 'The fire! Let's light the fire!'

'First I look,' said Kensuke. And, despite all my protestations, he went back into the cave house for his binoculars. I raced up the hill again. The junk was close enough to shore. They would be bound to see the smoke. I was sure of it. Kensuke was making his way up towards me infuriatingly slowly. He seemed to be in no hurry at all. He studied the boat carefully now through his binoculars, taking his time about it. 'We've got to light the fire,' I said. 'We've got to.'

Kensuke caught me suddenly by the arm. 'It is the same boat, Micasan. Killer men come. They kill the gibbons and steal away the babies. They come back again. I am very sure. I do not forget the boat. I never forget. They very wicked people. We must go quick. We must find all orang-utans. We must bring them into the cave. They be safe there.'

It did not take him long to gather them in. As we walked into the forest Kensuke simply began to sing.

They materialised out of nowhere, in twos, in threes, until we had fifteen of them. Four were still missing. We went deeper and deeper into the forest to find them, Kensuke singing all the while. Then three more came crashing through the trees, Tomodachi amongst them. Only one was still missing, Kikanbo.

Standing there in a clearing in the forest, surrounded by the orang-utans, Kensuke sang for Kikanbo again and again, but he did not come. Then we heard a motor start up, somewhere out at sea, an outboard motor. Kensuke sang out again louder now, more urgently. We listened for Kikanbo. We looked for him. We called for him.

'We cannot wait any longer,' said Kensuke at last. 'I go in front, Micason, you behind. Bring last ones with you. Quick now.' And off he went, up the track, leading one of the orang-utans by the hand, and still singing. As we followed, I remember thinking that this was just like the Pied Piper leading the children away into a cave in the mountain side.

I had my work cut out at the back. Some of the younger orang-utans were far more interested in playing hide-and-seek than following. In the end I had to scoop up two of them and carry them, one in the crook of each arm. They were a great deal heavier than they looked. I kept glancing back over my shoulder for Kikanbo, and calling for him, but he still did not come.

The outboard motor died. I heard voices, loud voices, men's voices, laughter. I was running now, the orang-utans clinging round my neck. The forest hooted and howled in alarm all around me.

As I reached the cave I heard the first shots ring out. Every bird, every bat in the forest lifted off so that the screeching sky was black with them. We gathered the orang-utans together at the back of the cave and huddled there in the darkness with them, as the shooting went on and on.

Of all of them, Tomodachi was the most agitated. But they all needed constant comfort and reassurance from Kensuke. All through this dreadful nightmare Kensuke sang to them softly.

The hunters were nearer, ever nearer, shooting and shouting. I closed my eyes. I prayed. The orang-utans whimpered aloud as if they were singing along with Kensuke. All this while Stella lay at my feet, a permanent growl in her throat. I held on to the ruff of her neck, just in case. The young orang-utans burrowed their heads into me wherever they could, under my arms, under my knees, and clung on.

The shots cracked so close now, splitting the air and echoing round the cave. There were distant yells of triumph. I knew only too well what this must mean.

After that the hunt moved away. We could hear no more voices, just the occasional shot. And then nothing. The forest had fallen silent. We stayed where we were for hours. I wanted to venture out to see if they had gone, but Kensuke would not let me. He sang all the time, and the orang-utans stayed huddled around us, until we heard the sound of the outboard motor starting up. Even then Kensuke still made me wait a while longer. When at last we did emerge, the junk was already well out to sea.

We searched the island for Kikanbo, sang for him, called for him, but there was no sign of him. Kensuke was in deep despair. He was inconsolable. He went off on his own and I let him go. I came across him shortly after, kneeling over the bodies of two dead gibbons, both mothers. He was not crying, but he had been. His eyes were filled with hurt and bewilderment. We dug away a hole in the soft earth on the edge of the forest and buried them. There were no words in me left to speak, and Kensuke had no songs left to sing.

We were making our sorrowful way back home along the beach when it happened. Kikanbo ambushed us. He came charging out of the trees, scattering sand at us and then climbed up Kensuke's leg and wrapped himself round his neck. It was such a good moment, a great moment.

That night Kensuke and I sang 'Ten Green Bottles' over and over again, very loudly, over our fish soup. It was, I suppose, a sort of wake for the two dead gibbons, as well as an ode to joy for Kikanbo. The forest outside seemed to echo our singing.

But in the weeks that followed I could see that Kensuke was brooding on the terrible events of that day. He set about making a cage of stout bamboo at the back of the cave to house the orang-utans more securely in case the killer men ever returned. He kept going over and over it, how he should have done this before, how he would never have forgiven himself if Kikanbo had been taken, how he wished the gibbons would come when he sang, so he could save them too. We cut down branches and brush from the forest and stacked them outside the cave mouth so that they could be pulled across to disguise the entrance to the cave house.

He became very nervous, very anxious, sending me often to the hilltop with the binoculars to see if the junk had returned. But as time went by, as the immediate threat receded, he became more his own self again. Even so, I felt he was always wary, always slightly on edge.

Because he was keeping so many of my paintings now, we found we were running out of good painting shells. So early one morning we set off on an expedition to find some more. We scoured the beach, heads down, side by side, just a few feet apart. There was always an element of competition with our shell collecting – who would find the first, the biggest, the most perfect. We had not been at it long and neither of us had yet found a single shell, when I became aware that he had stopped walking.

'Micasan,' he breathed, and he was pointing out to sea with his stick. There was something out there, something white, but too defined, too shaped, to be a cloud.

We had left the binoculars behind. With Stella yapping at me all the way, I raced back along the beach and up the track to the cave house, grabbed the binoculars and made for the top of the hill. A sail! Two sails. Two white sails. I bounded down the hillside, back into the cave and pulled out a lighted stick from the fire. By the time I reached the beacon Kensuke was already there. He took the binoculars from me and looked for himself.

'Can I light it?' I asked. 'Can I?'

'All right, Micasan,' he said. 'All right.'

I thrust the lighted stick deep into the beacon, in amongst the dry leaves and twigs at its core. It lit almost instantly and very soon flames were roaring up into the wood, licking out at us as the wind took them. We backed away at the sudden heat of it. I was disappointed there were so many flames. I wanted smoke, not flames. I wanted towering clouds of smoke.

'Do not worry, Micasan,' Kensuke said. 'They see this for sure. You see.'

We took turns with the binoculars. Still the yacht had not turned. They had not seen it. The smoke was beginning to billow up into the sky. Desperately I threw more and more wood onto the fire, until it was a roaring inferno of flame and dense smoke.

I had thrown on almost the very last of the wood we had collected, when Kensuke said suddenly, 'Micasan, it is coming. I think the boat is coming.'

He handed me the binoculars. The yacht was turning. It was very definitely turning, but I couldn't make out whether it was towards us or away from us. 'I don't know,' I said. 'I'm not sure.'

He took the binoculars off me. 'I tell you, Micasan, it come this way. They see us. I am very sure. It come to our island.'

Moments later, as the wind filled the sails, I knew he was right. We hugged each other there on the hilltop beside the blazing beacon. I leaped up and down like a wild thing, and Stella went mad with me. Every time I looked through the binoculars now, the yacht was coming in closer.

'She's a big yacht,' I said. 'I can't see her flag. Dark blue hull, like the *Peggy Sue*.' Only then, as I said

it out loud, did I begin to hope that it could possibly be her. Gradually hope turned to belief, and belief to certainty. I saw a blue cap, my mother's cap. It was them! It was them! 'Kensuke,' I cried, still looking through the binoculars, 'Kensuke, it's the *Peggy Sue*. It is. They've come back for me. They've come back.' But Kensuke did not reply. When I looked round, I discovered he was not there.

I found him sitting at the mouth of the cave house, with my football in his lap. He looked up at me, and I knew already from the look in his eyes what he was going to tell me.

He stood up, put his hands on my shoulders, and looked me deep in the eyes. 'You listen to me very good now, Micasan,' he said. 'I am too old for that new world you tell me about. It is very exciting world, but it is not my world. My world was Japan, long time ago. And now my world is here. I think about it for long time. If Kimi is alive, if Michiya is alive, then they think I am dead long time ago. I would be like ghost coming home. I am not same person. They not same either. And, besides, I have family here, orang-utan family. Maybe killer men come again. Who look after them then? No, I stay on my island. This is my place. This Kensuke's Kingdom. Emperor must stay in his Kingdom, look after his people. Emperor does not run away. Not honourable thing to do.'

I could see there was no point in pleading or arguing or protesting. He put his forehead against mine and let me cry. 'You go now,' he went on, 'but before you go, you promise three things. First, you paint every day of your life, so one day you be great artist like Hokusai. Second, you think of me sometime, often maybe, when you are home in England. When you look up at full moon, you think of me, and I do same for you. That way we never forget each other. Last thing you promise and very important for me. Very important you say nothing of this, nothing of me. You come here alone. You alone here in this place, you understand? I not here. After ten years, you say what you like. All that left of me then is bones. It not matter any more then. I want no one come looking for me. I stay here. I live life in peace. No people. People come, no peace. You understand? You keep secret for me, Mica? You promise?'

'I promise,' I said.

He smiled and gave me my football. 'You take football. You very good at football, but you very much better painter. You go now.' And with his arm round my shoulder he took me outside. 'You go,' he said. I walked away only a little way and turned round. He was still standing at the mouth of the cave. 'You go now please.' And he bowed to me. I bowed back. '*Sayonara*, Micasan', he said. 'It has been honour to know you, great honour of my life.' I hadn't the voice to reply.

Blinded with tears I ran off down the track. Stella didn't come at once, but by the time I reached the edge of the forest she had caught up with me. She raced out on to the beach barking at the *Peggy Sue*, but I stayed where I was hidden in the shadow of the trees and cried out all my tears. I watched the *Peggy Sue* come sailing in. It was indeed my mother and my father on-board. They had seen Stella by now and were calling to her. She was barking her silly head off. I saw the anchor go down.

'Goodbye, Kensuke,' I whispered. I took a deep breath and ran out on to the sand waving and yelling.

I splashed out into the shallows to meet them.

My mother just cried and hugged me till I thought I'd break. She kept saying over and over again, 'Didn't I tell you we'd find him? Didn't I tell you?'

The first words my father said were, 'Hello, monkey face.'

For almost a year my mother and father had searched for me. No one would help them, for no one would believe I could still be alive – not a chance in a million, they said. My father too – he later admitted – had given me up for dead. But never my mother. So far as she was concerned I was alive, I had to be alive. She simply knew it in her heart. So they had sailed from island to island, searching on until they had found me. Not a miracle, just faith.

Postscript

Four years after this book was first published, I received this letter.

Dear Michael,

I write to tell you, in my bad English, that my name is Michiya Ogawa. I am the son of Dr Kensuke Ogawa. Until I read your book I thought my father had died in the war. My mother died only three years ago still believing this. As you say in your book, we lived in Nagasaki, but we were very lucky. Before the bomb fell we went into the countryside to see my grandmother for a few days. So we lived.

I have no memories of my father, only some photographs and your book. It would be a pleasure to talk to someone who knew my father as you did. Maybe one day we could meet. I hope so.

With my best wishes,
Michiya Ogawa.

A month after receiving this letter I went to Japan, and I met Michiya. He laughs just like his father did.

ジ・エンド

Glossary

あぶない	*Abunai*	Danger!
アメリカ人	*Amerikajin*	An American
だめだ	*Dameda*	Forbidden
英国人	*Eikokujin*	An Englishman
ごめんなさい	*Gomenasai*	Sorry
ジャパン	. . . .	Japan
きかんぼう	*Kikanbo*	
きみ	*Kimi*	
道哉（みちや）	*Michiya*	
長崎	. . . .	Nagasaki
おやすみなさい	*Oyasumi nasai*	Goodnight
さよなら	*Sayonara*	Goodbye
ともだち	*Tomodachi*	
ジ・エンド	. . . .	The End
やめろ	*Yamero*	Stop!

Azores

La Coruña

Canaries

Cape Verde Is.

N.E. Tradewinds

The Doldrums

S.E. Trades

Recife

BRAZIL

St Helena

Rio de Janeiro

Westerlies

Cape T

---ROUTE OF PEGGY SUE---
SEPT. 20th 1987 — JULY 27th 1988

Papua
NEW
GUINEA

Coral Sea

AUSTRALIA

Barrier Reef

S.E. Trades

oPerth

oAdelaide   oSydney

Roaring Forties

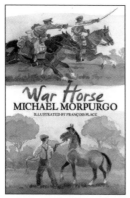
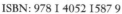
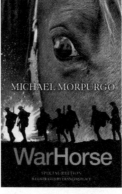

EGMONT PRESS: ETHICAL PUBLISHING

Egmont Press is about turning writers into successful authors and children into passionate readers – producing books that enrich and entertain. As a responsible children's publisher, we go even further, considering the world in which our consumers are growing up.

Safety First
Naturally, all of our books meet legal safety requirements. But we go further than this; every book with play value is tested to the highest standards – if it fails, it's back to the drawing-board.

Made Fairly
We are working to ensure that the workers involved in our supply chain – the people that make our books – are treated with fairness and respect.

Responsible Forestry
We are committed to ensuring all our papers come from environmentally and socially responsible forest sources.

**For more information, please visit our website at
www.egmont.co.uk/ethical**